The Professor's Advanced Book of Whimsy

Published by Michael C Petty
www.petty.org.uk

Cover and Illustrations by Brenda Nash
www.brendanash.co.uk
Design by Robert Simpson
www.squirclecreative.co.uk
Editing by Megan Whiting
www.meganwhiting.co.uk

First Printing, 2023

British Library Cataloguing-in-Publication Data
A catalogue record for this book is available from the British Library

ISBN 978-1-9996039-3-9
Published by Michael C Petty
www.petty.org.uk

Dedicated to my good friend
John E Fuller
1951-2023

CONTENTS

PREFACE

Humour is defined as the quality in something that makes you laugh. The term derives from the humoral medicine of the ancient Greeks, which taught that the balance of fluids in the human body, known as humours (Latin: humor, 'body fluid'), controlled our health and emotion. Laughter is often initiated by a joke. Freud argued that jokes can be categorised into the obscene (dirty jokes), aggressive (jokes that are considered in bad taste) or not funny. However, the richness of language, the sharpness of observations (in the forms of speech, writing and drawings) and situations give rise to many other forms of humour. Humour is often accompanied by wit, which has evolved to signify the quickness of mind and the ability to convey things in an amusing manner. Humour is perhaps a matter of observation and wit of expression.

The telling of jokes seems to be mainly a human activity, although there is a group of scientists, known as computation humourists, engaged in imparting a sense of humour to a machine. Good luck to them! Articulating a joke involves complex higher-order communication whereas laughter is a primitive instinct – a physical response halfway between fear and ecstasy – that we share with apes. Laughter is perceived in babies when they are about four months old. As soon as they begin to learn language, kids start to play with words. They are instinctively attracted to the nonsensical. Between the ages of about three and six, youngsters laugh abundantly at their own and others' funny stories and surreal imaginings. As they grow, they begin to distance themselves from their love of nonsense and take an interest in riddles. Telling jokes is a way for children to regain control of their surroundings, or at least alleviate their sense of frustration and impotence. My granddaughter told her first joke when she was three years old:

> Q: What did Baby Corn say to Mummy Corn?
> A: Where's Popcorn?

This shows a grasp of the English language, family relationships… and fast food.

Other common types of joke are based on stories, puzzles and riddles. Narrative jokes require a greater ability to tell, and it takes time to acquire this skill. Such humour is influential in certain religions. Riddles are used during meditation to help Zen Buddhists unravel truths about the world and themselves. The Zen teaching comes in the form of koans. These are little philosophical problems which, superficially at least, bear close resemblance to riddles. For instance:

> If a tree falls in a forest and there's no one there to hear, does it make a sound?

The answers are not always obvious. Ask a quantum physicist this question and they might say that the sound was there – but you couldn't be sure that the tree was!

As for the best joke of all, in 2001, an internet site invited people of all ages and nationalities to submit their favourite joke, and rate how funny they found a random selection of jokes. Over 40,000 were sent in from around the world, evaluated by 350,000 people. The result was the world's funniest joke, albeit chosen by committee. It later turned out to be based on a 1951 Goon Show sketch by Spike Milligan:

> Two hunters are out in the woods when one of them collapses. He doesn't seem to be breathing and his eyes are rolled back in his head.

> The other man takes out his phone and calls the emergency services. He gasps, *"My friend is dead! What can I do?"* The operator says, *"Calm down. I can help. First, let's make sure he's dead."* There is a silence; then a gunshot is heard. Back on the phone, the man says, *"OK, now what?"*

Not bad, I suppose. But, in my opinion, the finest joke ever must be The Monkey Joke. This is a visual joke (ideally told by a Geordie) and sadly cannot appear in the pages of this book. Some things must remain a mystery.

Following the successful Professor's Book of Whimsy, here is a further collection of jokes, stories and puzzles, with delightful illustrations by the artist Brenda Nash. The 'whimsy' badge reflects the somewhat capricious nature of the compilation. Jokes generally have no author (although pinching jokes from professional comedians is no longer considered a homage). They circulate in mysterious ways and are a barometer of the social and political climate at that time. Mostly, the jokes here are unaccredited. Where I have been able to identify an author, I have. My sincere apologies if any injustices have been done.

Michael C Petty
County Durham, UK
July 2023

AGE CANNOT WITHER HER

A Northern Inheritance

Geordie is on his last legs; he knows the end is near. He gathers his wife, two sons and daughter to his bedside. As he is about to pass on his legacy, he asks two neighbours to act as witnesses.

"Now then, bairn," he says to his daughter, Cheryl, *"please take the row of terraced hooses in Jesmond."*

"Oh Da, thank you sooo much," says Cheryl.

Turning to his son, Anthony,

"And you can take the office block in the toon."

Then it was Declan's turn.

"You can take all the apartments in Gateshead."

"Wey eye," exclaims the son.

Finally, Geordie beckons to his wife.

"Bonny lass, please take the seafront hotel in Whitley Bay."

Geordie finally slips away.

The neighbours are both stunned to hear of Geordie's vast wealth. They had known him for many years and were under the impression he didn't have two pennies to rub together.

Addressing Geordie's wife, one remarks,

"My condoolences for your loss, but Geordie must have been such a harworking and woonderful man to amass that portfolio of property?"

"Howay, man," says the wife, *"he wer not rich. He jus had a big window cleaning round."*

You Are Old, Father William

Lewis Carroll, Alice's Adventures in Wonderland, 1865

"You are old, Father William," the young man said,
"And your hair has become very white;
And yet you incessantly stand on your head –
Do you think, at your age, it is right?"

"In my youth," Father William replied to his son,
"I feared it might injure the brain;
But now that I'm perfectly sure I have none,
Why, I do it again and again."

"You are old," said the youth, "as I mentioned before,
And have grown most uncommonly fat;
Yet you turned a back-somersault in at the door –
Pray, what is the reason of that?"

"In my youth," said the sage, as he shook his grey locks,
"I kept all my limbs very supple
By the use of this ointment – one shilling a box –
Allow me to sell you a couple?"

"You are old," said the youth, "and your jaws are too weak
For anything tougher than suet;
Yet you finished the goose, with the bones and the beak –
Pray, how did you manage to do it?"

"In my youth," said his father, "I took to the law,
And argued each case with my wife;
And the muscular strength which it gave to my jaw,
Has lasted the rest of my life."

"You are old," said the youth, "one would hardly suppose
That your eye was as steady as ever;
Yet you balanced an eel on the end of your nose –
What made you so awfully clever?"

"I have answered three questions, and that is enough,"
Said his father; "don't give yourself airs!
Do you think I can listen all day to such stuff?
Be off, or I'll kick you down stairs!"

Copying Errors

An old monk arrives at a monastery where his younger colleagues spend their time making copies of the ancient books that underpin their order.

The old monk goes to the basement of the monastery, saying he wants to make copies of the original documents rather than facsimiles made by others, to avoid duplicating errors that might have occurred.

Several hours later, the monks, wondering where their new friend is, find him sobbing in the basement. They ask him what is wrong and he says, *"the word is celebrate, not celibate!"*

Money for Nothing

An astute old man has become very bored in retirement and decides to open his own medical practice. He puts a sign up outside his house: 'Dr Geezer's Consultations. Get your treatment for £500. Results guaranteed or receive £1,000.'

Dr Pipsqueak is convinced this is a scam. Nevertheless, he thinks it will be a great opportunity to make a quick £1,000, so he goes to Dr Geezer's clinic.

Dr Pipsqueak: *"Dr Geezer, I have lost all sense of taste. Can you help?"*

Dr Geezer: *"Nurse, please bring medicine from box 22 and put three drops on Dr Pipsqueak's tongue."*

Dr Pipsqueak: *"Aaagh!! This is petrol!"*

Dr Geezer: *Congratulations! You've got your taste back. That will be £500."*

Dr Pipsqueak is annoyed and returns after a couple of days, determined to recover his money.

Dr Pipsqueak: *"I have lost my memory; I cannot remember anything."*

Dr Geezer: *"Nurse, please bring medicine from box 22 and put three drops on Dr Pipsqueak's tongue."*

Dr Pipsqueak: *"Oh, no you don't... that is petrol!"*

Dr Geezer: *"Congratulations! You've got your memory back. That will be £500."*

Dr Pipsqueak (having lost £1,000) leaves angrily and comes back a week later.

Dr Pipsqueak: *"My eyesight has become weak – I can no longer see clearly."*

Dr Geezer: *"Unfortunately, I don't have any medicine for that condition. Here's your £1,000 back."*

He gives him £100 in cash.

Dr Pipsqueak: *"But this is only £100!"*

Dr Geezer: *"Congratulations! You have your vision back! That will be £500."*

Once Upon a Time...

On a remote island in the South Pacific lived a tribe of proud warriors. Their King was much loved and reigned supreme, but he was always on the lookout for how he might enhance his status.

One day, while wandering by the ocean, the King chanced upon a book that had been washed ashore. It turned out to be a catalogue from John Lewis, the famous London department store. The King left the catalogue to dry out on the beach, and later took it back to his hut to read about the goods on offer.

There was some fabulous merchandise. A large, ornate, upright chair particularly attracted the King, who was also very taken by the John Lewis reputation for value for money and their ability for international delivery.

This would make an excellent throne, thought the King. It will be perfect for my grass hut.

A couple of months later, the 'throne' arrived. It was truly enormous, and once installed in the King's hut, there was little room for anything else.

The King came up with a plan. He got his trusty tribesmen to attach some long ropes to the throne. In this way, it could be hoisted to the ceiling of the King's hut at night and secured on a large hook, so that he could sleep in his bed below.

The scheme worked well. In the morning, the King would arise, and his loyal subjects would move his bed and then lower the throne, ready for the day's activities. And after dinner, the throne would be hoisted to the ceiling and replaced by the King's bed.

Then the autumn storms arrived. One night, the rains were incessant. The water penetrated the King's grass hut and significantly weakened the roof… and the hook holding the throne.

Finally, the hook came out of its fastening, and John Lewis' finest furniture fell onto the incumbent King.

He was unceremoniously crushed to death.

The tribesmen were distraught and mourned their King for many years.

They devised a cautionary warning to others, which was inscribed on the King's headstone – an adage that is now commonplace throughout the world:

'People who live in grass houses shouldn't store thrones.'

Time Watching

Dave Allen

We are servants of time. We spend our lives by the clock. We are brought up to respect the clock. Punctuality is everything. We get up by the clock, eat and sleep by the clock, get up again with the clock, go to work, clock-in, clock-out – and then, after forty years, we retire. And what do they give us? A bloody clock!

Sharing and Caring

An old man and his wife visit their local branch of McDonald's. The man orders a single burger, small fries and a cup of tea. He unwraps the plain beef burger and cuts it in half, placing one half in front of his wife.

He then carefully counts out the chips, dividing them into two piles, and neatly places one pile in front of his wife. He takes a sip of the tea, his wife takes a sip, and then he sets the cup down between them.

As the man takes a few bites of his half of the burger, the people around them are looking over and whispering. Clearly, they are thinking, That poor old couple – all they can afford is one meal between them.

As the man begins to eat his fries, a young customer comes up to the table and politely offers to buy another meal for the old couple. The man says that they are just fine; they are used to sharing everything.

Customers closer to the table notice that the old lady hasn't eaten a bite. She sits there watching her husband, and they occasionally take turns sipping the tea.

Again, the young man comes over and begs them to let him buy another meal. This time it is the lady who says, "*No thank you, we are used to sharing everything.*"

Finally, as the man finishes his food and is wiping his face with a napkin, the young man again comes over to the old lady, who has yet to eat a single morsel of food, and says, "*I am a bit concerned. Why haven't you eaten anything? What is it you are waiting for?*"

She answers, "*The teeth.*"

The Old Ones Are the Best Ones

In search of the oldest joke ever written down, I came across a candidate in the book by Jimmy Carr and Lucy Greeves (The Naked Jape, Penguin, 2006).

It comes from the Greek text Philogelos, meaning 'the laughter-lover'; a collection of 265 jokes put together in 4 or 5 AD. Many of the 'jokes' translate poorly to modern times, but here is one that might ring true:

Someone provoked a well-known wit: "*I had your wife, without paying a penny.*"

He replied: "*It's my duty as a husband to couple with such a monstrosity. What made you do it?*"

Perhaps, this might be updated...

A woman comes home and finds her best friend in bed with her husband. The woman throws up her hands in disbelief, saying, "*Hey Emma, I have to – but you?*"

Public Announcement

A man goes into a confession booth and tells the priest, *"Father, I'm seventy-five years old, and last night I made love to two twenty-year-old girls – at the same time."*

The priest gasps and says, *"When did you last go to confession?"*

The man says, *"I have never been to confession, Father. I'm Jewish."*

The priest says, *"Then why are you telling me?"*

The man replies, *"I'm telling everyone."*

Fond Memories

A group of lads, all turning forty, chat about where they should gather for their celebratory lunch. It is agreed they will go to The Crown in Croydon, because this is where they congregated as teenagers and dated their first girlfriends.

Ten years later, the friends deliberate where they should meet for lunch. They resolve to visit The Crown in Croydon, because the waitresses are attractive, the food is good, as is the service, and the beer selection is excellent.

Another ten years pass, and the lads are now sixty. They again consider where they should convene. The friends settle on The Crown in Croydon, because there is plenty of parking, they can dine in peace and quiet, with no loud music, and it is good value for money.

Ten years pass and the group are now seventy. The friends discuss where they should meet for lunch. They choose The Crown in Croydon, because the restaurant is wheelchair accessible and has a toilet for the disabled.

The lads are still around ten years later and, at the ripe old age of eighty, consider where they should go for their anniversary meal. The location is obvious. They will meet at The Crown in Croydon – it has an excellent reputation, and they have never been before.

THE CROWN

Put Another Way

William Shakespeare, As You Like It, 1599

"All the world's a stage,
And all the men and women merely players;
They have their exits and their entrances,
And one man in his time plays many parts,
His acts being seven ages. At first, the infant,
Mewling and puking in the nurse's arms.
Then the whining schoolboy, with his satchel
And shining morning face, creeping like snail
Unwillingly to school. And then the lover,
Sighing like furnace, with a woeful ballad
Made to his mistress' eyebrow. Then a soldier,
Full of strange oaths and bearded like the pard,
Jealous in honour, sudden and quick in quarrel,
Seeking the bubble reputation
Even in the cannon's mouth. And then the justice,
In fair round belly with good capon lined,
With eyes severe and beard of formal cut,
Full of wise saws and modern instances;
And so he plays his part. The sixth age shifts
Into the lean and slippered pantaloon,
With spectacles on nose and pouch on side;
His youthful hose, well saved, a world too wide
For his shrunk shank, and his big manly voice,
Turning again toward childish treble, pipes
And whistles in his sound. Last scene of all,
That ends this strange eventful history,
Is second childishness and mere oblivion,
Sans teeth, sans eyes, sans taste, sans everything."

Five Secrets

The five secrets to a perfect relationship:

- it's important to find a partner who works around the house, cooks, cleans and who has a job;
- it's important to find a partner who makes you laugh;
- it's important to find a partner who is dependable, respectful, and doesn't lie;
- it's important to find a partner who's good in bed; and
- it is essential that these four partners never meet.

Conundrum A

In 2016, the UK EastEnders actor Danny Dyer revealed, in a television programme, that he was a direct descendant of King Edward III of England (1312–1377), who was Danny's 22 times great grandfather. A simple calculation suggests that Danny would have approximately 16 million people who would also be his 22 times great grandparents (based on two parents, four grandparents, eight great grandparents, 16 two times great grandparents and so on… up to 2 to the power 24 or 2^{24} for Danny's 22 times grandparents).

This number is greater than the population of England during the fourteenth century. In fact, a similar calculation reveals that a single individual alive today would, over thirty generations, going back to the Middle Ages, have 2^{30} or roughly a billion ancestors; more than the total world population at the time.

How is this paradox explained?

EXIT PURSUED BY A BEAR

Hartlepool Hominid

One stormy day during the Napoleonic Wars, a French ship was wrecked off the coast of an old fishing village clinging to the north-east coast of England.

The only survivor was the ship's mascot, a monkey, which was washed ashore. The people of Hartlepool had never seen a monkey before – nor, for that matter, had they ever set eyes on a Frenchman. Mistaking the monkey's chattering for the language of the enemy, they convicted the monkey of being a French spy and hanged the animal on the beach.

Or so the story goes…

Whatever the truth, the legend of Hartlepool and the hanged monkey has endured for over 200 years.

Over the centuries, the folklore has been used to taunt the Hartlepudlians. Most residents, however, love this story. H'Angus the Monkey is the official mascot of Hartlepool United, the local football team. The successful mayoral candidate in the 2002 local elections, Stuart Drummond, campaigned dressed in the costume of H'Angus, using the election slogan 'free bananas for schoolchildren' – a promise he was unfortunately unable to keep. However, this appears not to have dented his popularity, as he went on to be re-elected twice.

I Wonder Why?

Two lions are walking down an aisle in Sainsbury's.

One turns to the other and says, *"Quiet in here today, isn't it?"*

Slow

A family of tortoises venture into their local ice cream parlour for a treat. They order, sit down, and are about to indulge in their ice creams when the father tortoise says, *"I think it's going to rain. Junior, will you pop back home and fetch my umbrella?"*

So off goes Junior, but three days later, he still hasn't returned.

Eventually, the mother tortoise turns to the father and says, *"I think we had better eat Junior's ice cream before it melts."*

And a voice from the door says, *"If you do that, I won't go."*

And Slower

Did you hear about the racing snail who got rid of his shell?

He thought this would make him faster, but it just made him sluggish.

Wasp Whiz

The world's leading expert on European wasps walks into a record shop.

He asks the assistant, *"Do you have European Vespidae Acoustics Volume 2? I believe it was released this week."*

ICE CREAM PARLOUR
FOR SALE
15
SPEEDY SLUG

"Certainly," replies the assistant. *"Perhaps you would like to listen before you make a purchase?"*

"Wonderful," says the expert, and puts on a pair of headphones.

He listens for a few moments, then says to the assistant, *"I'm terribly sorry, but I am the world's leading expert on European wasps, and this is not accurate at all. I don't recognise any of these sounds. Are you sure this is the correct recording?"*

The assistant checks the turntable and replies that it is indeed European Vespidae Acoustics Volume 2. The assistant apologises and moves the stylus onto the next track.

Again, the expert listens for a few moments and then says to the assistant, *"No, this just can't be right! I've been an expert in this field for forty-three years and I am not familiar with any of this."*

The assistant apologises once again and transfers the needle to the next track.

The expert throws off the headphones as soon as it starts playing and is fuming.

"This is outrageous, misleading advertising! I am the world's leading expert on European wasps, and no European wasp has ever made a sound like those on this record!"

The manager of the shop overhears the commotion and walks over.

"What appears to be the problem, sir?"

"I am the world's leading expert on European wasps. Nobody knows more about them than I do. There is no way that the sounds on this record were made by European wasps!"

The manager glances down and identifies the problem instantly.

"I'm so sorry, sir. It seems we've been playing you the B side."

Barry's Ultimate Parrot Joke

Barry Cryer

A woman goes to a pet shop and sees a parrot on sale for £5.

"It came from a brothel," says the shopkeeper, *"and, to put it politely, it has quite an extensive vocabulary."*

"Never mind," says the woman. *"At that price, I'll take it."*

So she takes the parrot home, puts its cage in the living room and takes the cover off.

"New place – very nice," says the parrot.

Then the woman's two daughters walk in.

"New place, new girls – very nice," says the parrot.

Then the woman's husband walks in, and the parrot says, *"Oh hello, Keith."*

The High Life

An eagle was sitting at the top of a tall tree, doing nothing. A small rabbit saw the eagle and asked, *"Can I also sit like you and do nothing?"*

The eagle answered: *"Sure, why not?"*

So, the rabbit sat on the ground below the eagle and rested.

Suddenly, a fox appeared, jumped on the rabbit, and ate it.

Moral of the story:

To be sitting and doing nothing, you must be sitting very, very high up.

The Owl and the Pussy-Cat

Edward Lear, 1871

I

The Owl and the Pussy-cat went to sea
In a beautiful pea-green boat,
They took some honey, and plenty of money,
Wrapped up in a five-pound note.
The Owl looked up to the stars above,
And sang to a small guitar,
"O lovely Pussy! O Pussy, my love,
What a beautiful Pussy you are,
You are,
You are!
What a beautiful Pussy you are!"

II

Pussy said to the Owl, "You elegant fowl!
How charmingly sweet you sing!
O let us be married! too long we have tarried:
But what shall we do for a ring?"
They sailed away, for a year and a day,
To the land where the Bong-Tree grows
And there in a wood a Piggy-wig stood
With a ring at the end of his nose,
His nose,
His nose,
With a ring at the end of his nose.

III

"Dear Pig, are you willing to sell for one shilling
Your ring?" Said the Piggy, "I will."
So they took it away, and were married next day
By the Turkey who lives on the hill.
They dined on mince, and slices of quince,
Which they ate with a runcible spoon;
And hand in hand, on the edge of the sand,
They danced by the light of the moon,
The moon,
The moon,
They danced by the light of the moon.

Approximation

After a sheepdog gets all the sheep into a pen, he reports back to the farmer: *"All forty accounted for."*

"But I only have thirty-six sheep," says the farmer.

"I know," says the sheepdog. *"But I rounded them up."*

Fly for Sale

A man walks into a pet shop and says to the shop assistant, *"Can I have a pet fly, please?"*

The shop assistant replies, *"I'm sorry sir, we only have the usual pets here, like cats, dogs, rabbits and budgies. We don't sell flies."*

"That's odd," says the man. *"I'm sure I saw one in the window yesterday."*

Not Endangered

A man is in court, accused of killing a golden eagle.

The magistrate says: *"This is a dreadful act. Are there any mitigating circumstances?"*

The man responds, *"I am terribly sorry. I did not intend to kill the bird. I was shooting pheasants and the eagle flew into my line of fire. It was an unavoidable accident."*

The magistrate replies, *"Under the circumstances, I will let you off with a warning. As a matter of interest, what did you do with the eagle?"*

"I ate it," says the man.

"And what did it taste like?"

"Rather like swan."

Bradford Banter

A Yorkshireman walks into a vet and says, *"Ay up, can tha tek a look at our cat? It's not bin its sen lately."*

"Sure," says the vet. *"First things first. Is it a Tom?"*

"Nah," he replies. *"I've got it 'ere wi me."*

A Danger to Himself

As a postman is walking up the drive of a country house, he spots a sign: 'Danger! Beware of Dog'.

Close to the front door, he sees a harmless old Labrador asleep in the middle of the path.

"Is that the dog I'm supposed to beware of?" he asks the owner.

"That's him," comes the reply.

"He doesn't look dangerous to me. Why did you put up that sign?"

"Before I put up the sign, people kept tripping over him."

Conundrum B

Does a delivery van carrying pigeons weigh less if the birds are flying?

IN NATURE'S INFINITE BOOK OF SECRECY

Teaching Defined

Lewis Carroll, Alice's Adventures in Wonderland, 1865

"And how many hours a day did you do lessons?" said Alice, in a hurry to change the subject.

"Ten hours the first day," said the Mock Turtle: *"nine the next, and so on."*

"What a curious plan!" exclaimed Alice.

"That's the reason they're called lessons," the Gryphon remarked: *"because they lessen from day to day."*

Examination Evolution

Adapted from The American Mathematical Monthly, Vol. 101, No. 5, May 1994

1950s: A farmer sells a bag of onions for £10. His costs amount to 4/5 of his selling price. What is his profit?

1980s:	A farmer sells a bag of onions for £10. His costs amount to 4/5 of his selling price, that is, £8. What is his profit?
2000s:	A farmer sells a bag of onions for £10. His or her production costs are £8, and his or her profit is £2. Draw a diagram of an onion. Label this fully.
2020s:	An agricultural operative sells a consignment of organic onions for £10. Their production costs are 0.80 of their revenue. Run the ONION program on your laptop to determine the profit. Write a brief essay that analyses this example in the real world of economics.

God's Particle?

A Higgs boson walks into a Catholic church, and the priest asks, *"Why did you come in here?"*

The boson replies, *"Are you kidding? You can't have mass without me!"*

Heads in the Clouds

Two theoretical physicists are lost at the top of a mountain. The first opens a map and peruses it for a while, then he turns to the other physicist and says:

"Hey, I've figured it out. I know exactly where we are."

"Where are we then?"

"Do you see that mountain over there?"

"Yes."

"Well… THAT'S where we are."

Mathematical Manipulation

John von Neumann, the famous mathematician and computer scientist, once said:

"With four parameters I can fit an elephant, and with five I can make him wiggle his trunk."

By this, he meant that one should not be impressed when a complex mathematical model fits a data set well. With sufficient parameters, you can fit any set of data.

Collective Callings

Adapted from the Journal of Irreproducible Results, Volume 1, 1965

A grid of electrical engineers

A field of theoretical physicists

An amalgamation of metallurgists

A galaxy of cosmologists

A litter of geneticists

A set of mathematicians

A stack of librarians

A cloud of meteorologists

A dissonance of professors

A complex of psychologists

A colony of bacteriologists

A chain of prison officers

A wing of ornithologists

The Liar Paradox

Consider the sentence,

'This sentence is false.'

If we say the sentence is true, then it is false. If we say it is false, then it is true. Linguists and philosophers have long pondered this illogicality, but it remains an enigma.

Chemical Threat

There is increasing worldwide concern about the safety of the ubiquitous chemical dihydrogen monoxide (DHMO). This is a known causal component in many thousands of deaths. Dihydrogen monoxide is colourless, odourless, tasteless, and is a major contributor to billions of pounds in damage to property and the environment. Symptoms of DHMO ingestion can include excessive sweating and urination, nausea, vomiting, and body electrolyte imbalance. For those who have become dependent, DHMO withdrawal means certain death.

Some of the known hazards are:

- death due to accidental inhalation of DHMO, even in small quantities
- severe tissue damage after prolonged exposure to solid DHMO
- serious burns when exposed to gaseous DHMO
- short-circuits when electrical systems are contaminated

Furthermore, DHMO leads to corrosion and oxidation of many metals, is a major component of acid rain, and contributes to soil erosion. The chemical is also found in biopsies of pre-cancerous tumours and lesions.

Yet the chemical is present in every river, stream, lake and reservoir throughout the world.

Should we be concerned? And is it now time for the usage of dihydrogen monoxide to be regulated?

Fundamental Laws

First Law of Thermodynamics: You can't win.

Second Law of Thermodynamics: You can't break even.

Chicken Run

Adapted from an original yarn by Ken Dodd, and with apologies to Kenneth Grahame

The University of Pizza (the 'Fast-Food' university) is in the north of England. Owain Jenkins has recently accepted a position as Head of Course Quality.

Jenkins' eyes first met those of Ms Montmorency (Pro-Vice-Chancellor for Teaching) at the faculty review of Supermarket Studies. The relationship had been consummated shortly afterwards in the Blodgett Room in Old Pepperoni Hall – ostensibly whilst checking though student evaluations from the Department of Biscuits and Cookies. They were an odd couple: Jenkins, vertically challenged and from a council estate somewhere near Cardiff, while Montmorency was over six foot and hailed from good, upper-class breeding stock in Oxford.

None of this mattered to Jenkins, who was in love, and, on a sweltering summer Sunday, was taking Montmorency for a spin in his 1956 Morris Minor. The Porthcawl male choir was on the radio, tunefully singing the well-known folk ditty Ctfri'r Giefr (Counting the Goats). Everything was just perfect.

As they rounded a bend in the road, a familiar figure came into view.

Montmorency was the first to react.

"Look, darling – there's Professor Skimbleshanks on his bike. Let's get the bastard."

What a remarkable and commanding woman, thought Jenkins. And she was right about Skimbleshanks. He was a thorn in the side of his Course Quality department. What right did he, a mere member of the academic staff, have to interfere with Jenkins' own carefully orchestrated bureaucratic procedures?

Jenkins put his foot to the floor and the car responded with sonorous drone. In an instant (as it seemed) Skimbleshanks was in the ditch, entangled in spokes, tyres and pedals. Meanwhile, the Morris headed out of town and onto the dual carriageway. Life was indeed wonderful. The choir was by now well into the second verse of Ei Bendith ar ei Ben (God Bless the Prince of Wales).

After a while, Jenkins sensed some sort of action in the road behind. In the rear-view mirror, he saw a small cloud of dust, with a dark centre of energy, advancing on the Morris at incredible speed. A faint *"cluck-cluck"* could just be discerned above the engine noise. Hardly regarding it, Jenkins had turned to resume his conversation with Ms Montmorency, when suddenly the peaceful scene changed. Jenkins' mirror was now filled with the reflections from a white mass – and a chicken promptly overtook him. *"Cluck-Cluck. CLUCK-CLUCK."*

This was no ordinary bird – it had three legs. Jenkins had little time to assimilate the bizarre scene as he was quickly overtaken again, this time by a Bentley, driven by Old Gumby, the Vice-Chancellor's chauffeur, valet, and odd-job person. It was evident that Old Gumby was in hot pursuit of the three-legged chicken.

Jenkins was intrigued and decided to follow. He increased his pace. Through the Pizza countryside the trio flew: the three-legged chicken followed closely by Old Gumby and, some way behind, Jenkins and Montmorency. The thrill of the chase had a mesmerising effect on Jenkins. He sang as he motored – Rhyfelgyrch Gwyr Harlech – and the miles were eaten up under him. As all 803 ccs of the engine devoured the open country, he was only conscious that he was Jenkins, the High Priest of Quality Assurance, Jenkins at his best, Jenkins the lover, Jenkins the terror, the traffic queller.

Many miles later, the convoy's speed dropped, and Jenkins emerged from his trance to the solemn tones of Hen Wlad fy Nhadau. The terrain had become familiar; this was Gnocchi, a run-down suburb of Pizza. Through careful study of the council minutes, Jenkins had learned that here was the location of the university's latest venture – a new college focusing on a range of exciting projects. He had also heard that Professor Mistoffelees – internationally acclaimed expert on the cheeseburger and the previous Vice-Chancellor – had been brought out of retirement to head some important enterprise in Gnocchi.

The chicken slowed as it reached the entrance to what seemed to be a chemical plant. Above the wrought iron gates, Jenkins could clearly read the inscription:

'University of Pizza (Gnocchi Campus) – Genetically Engineered Fast-Food Laboratories.'

Jenkins pulled up behind the Bentley as the three-legged chicken disappeared up an alleyway between two buildings. And, sure enough, there was Mistoffelees – looking somewhat harassed.

As Mistoffelees approached, Jenkins lowered the window.

"I am naturally delighted to see you, Professor Mistoffelees. But what is going on here?"

"The VC's idea. He obtained substantial government funding for regional technology transfer in the arena of genetically modified food."

"But there is another, very pragmatic, reason," Mistoffelees continued. *"When it comes to his Sunday roast, the VC likes a chicken leg, his wife likes a leg, and Old Gumby also likes a leg, so a three-legged chicken seemed to satisfy an important local need."*

"Inspirational!" toadied Jenkins. *"And how does this genetically-modified bird taste?"*

"Therein lies a problem. I am afraid that we have yet to catch one."

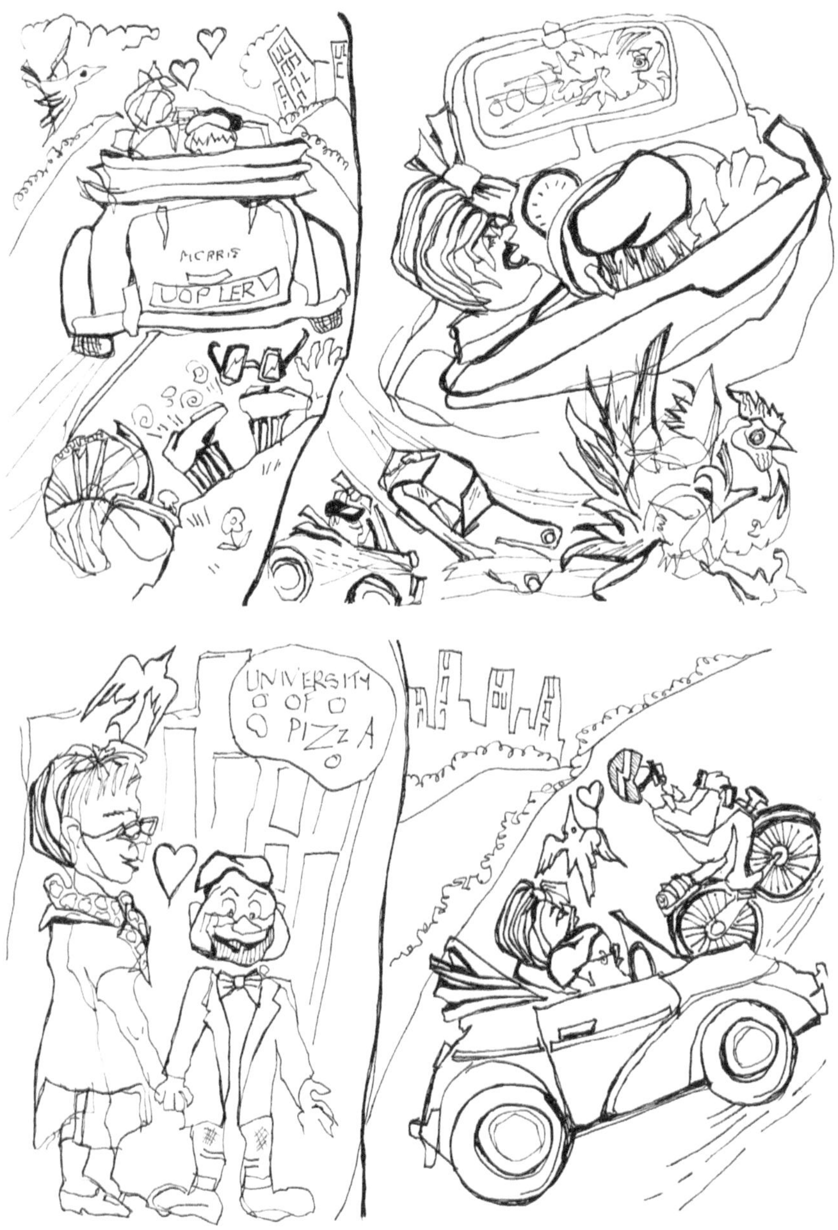
MORRIS
UOP LER
UNIVERSITY
OF
PIZZA

Comedy of Errors

This sentence contains exactly threee erors.

Anticipating the Lecture

Barry Cryer

There's an old man walking along the street at two in the morning. He's staggering a bit and holding a glass. So the police stop him and ask him where he's going.

"*To a lecture,*" says the man.

"*At two in the morning?*" asks the policeman. "*What's the lecture on?*"

"*Smoking and drinking,*" the old man replies.

"*Who's giving it?*"

"*My wife.*"

Memory Jogger

If you are in the habit of forgetting your four-digit PIN, here is a code that does not have to be memorised as it can always be calculated.

Choose any four-digit number and re-arrange the digits to create the largest and also the smallest possible numbers. Subtract the smallest from the largest to produce another four-digit number and simply repeat the procedure no more than eight times until the PIN is repeated and thus revealed.

The magic number will always be 6174, whatever numbers you choose, and is known as Kapreka's Constant, named after the Indian mathematician, D R Kapreka, who discovered this in 1949.

But, don't tell anyone!

Intelligent Lifeform?

In deep space, two aliens are engaged in conversation.

First alien: *"The dominant life forms on the Earth planet have developed satellite-based nuclear weapons."*

Second alien: *"Are they an emerging intelligence?"*

First alien: *"I don't think so… they have the weapons aimed at themselves."*

Pragmatism

An optimist will tell you that a glass is half full.

A pessimist will tell you that a glass is half empty.

But an engineer will tell you that the glass is twice the size it needs to be.

Different Points of View

Why did the chicken cross the road? Our greatest thinkers have divergent opinions:

Aristotle:	*"It is the nature of chickens to cross roads."*
Isaac Newton:	*"Chickens at rest tend to stay at rest, chickens in motion tend to cross roads."*
Albert Einstein:	*"Whether the chicken crossed the road, or the road moved beneath the chicken, depends on your frame of reference."*
Werner Heisenberg:	*"We are not sure which side of the road the chicken was on, but it was moving very fast."*
Wolfgang Pauli:	*"There was already a chicken on this side of the road."*

All you need is

$$y = \frac{1}{x}$$

$$x^2 + y^2 = 9$$

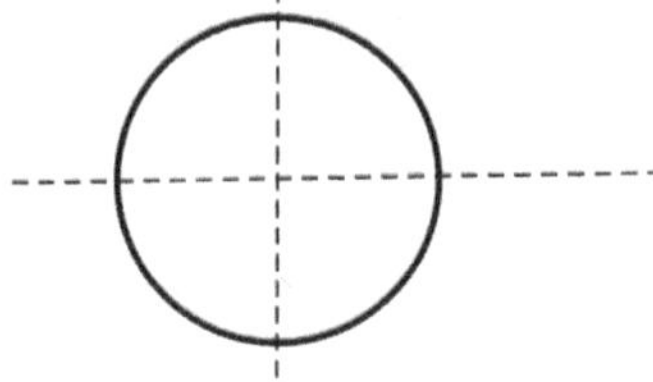

$$y = |-2x|$$

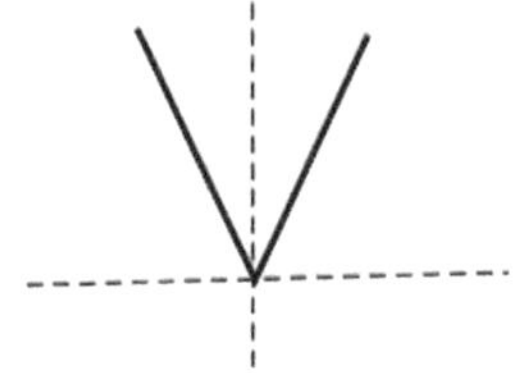

$$x = -3|\sin y|$$

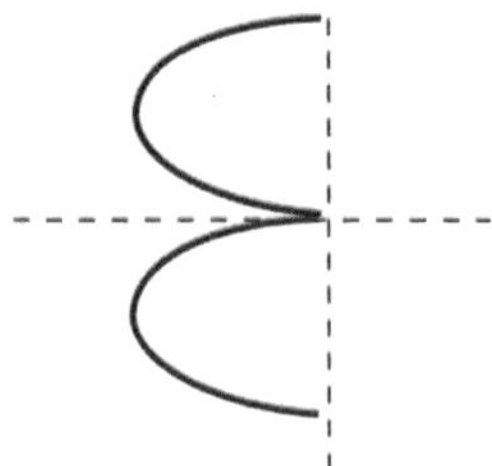

Under Pressure

Einstein, Newton and Pascal are having a scientific discussion.

Einstein becomes bored, so suggests, *"Let's play hide-and-seek. I'll be 'it'."*

The others agree, so Einstein begins counting. *"One... Two... Three..."*

Pascal runs off straight away to find a place to hide, but Newton merely takes out a piece of chalk and draws a one metre by one metre square on the ground. He finishes and steps into the square just as Einstein shouts, *"Ready or not - here I come!"*

Einstein looks up and immediately spots Newton standing in front of him.

He says, *"I have found you, Pascal!"*

Approaches To Life

An engineer thinks that his equations approximate reality. A physicist thinks reality approximates his equations. A mathematician doesn't care.

Natural Selection

A herd of wildebeest can move only as fast as the slowest animal. When the herd is hunted, it is the slowest and weakest members at the back that are killed first. This natural selection is good for the herd, because the general speed and health of the whole group keeps improving by regular killing of the weakest members.

In much the same way, the human brain can only operate as fast as the slowest brain cells. Excessive intake of alcohol, we all know, kills brain cells, but naturally it attacks the slowest and weakest cells first. Regular consumption of beer therefore eliminates the weaker brain cells, making the brain a faster and more efficient machine.

That is the reason you always feel cleverer after a few beers, and that's why a pint of beer is so good for you.

Alternative Prizes

The Ig Nobel Prizes are awarded annually, at a ceremony in Harvard University, to celebrate ten unusual triumphs in scientific research. The stated aim is to 'honour achievements that first make people laugh, and then make them think'. The title of the award is a pun on the Nobel Prize, which it parodies, and on the word ignoble (not noble). The awards were created in 1991 by Marc Abrahams, editor and co-founder of the Annals of Improbable Research, and a former editor-in-chief of the Journal of Irreproducible Results. Although the focus is on fun, there is a serious side to these awards. Unorthodox, even absurd, thinking is sometimes needed for science to progress. Here are a few of the past winners…

1996 – Tumbling Toast

The 1996 Prize in Physics went to Robert Matthews of Aston University for his paper Tumbling toast, Murphy's law and the fundamental constants, which sought to explain why toast tends to fall buttered side down.

1998 – Footsteps of Progress

The myth that there is a connection between the size of someone's shoes and the length of their penis is a pervasive one. Folk wisdom dictates that big shoes equate to a bigger penis, but what does science have to say? Jerald Bain of Mount Sinai Hospital in Toronto and Kerry Siminoski of the University of Alberta took on the challenge of investigating the truth of this age-old innuendo. Their research paper, The relationships among height, penile length, and foot size, established that shoe size was no indicator of manhood, and won them the 1998 Prize in Statistics.

1999 – A Good Year for Tea

There was a tie for the 1999 Prize in Physics. Len Fisher of the University of Bristol calculated the best possible way to dunk a biscuit in tea. In somewhat related research, Jean-Marc Vanden-Broeck of the University of East Anglia and Joseph Keller of Sanford University earned the honour by devising a nondrip teapot spout.

2000 – Flying Frogs

Sir Andre Geim (University of Nijmegen) and Sir Michael Berry (University of Bristol) were awarded the 2000 Prize in Physics for levitating a frog with magnets. Geim went on to win the (actual) Nobel Prize in Physics a decade later for graphene research, making him the only person to have won both the Ig Nobel Prize and the Nobel Prize.

2002 – Cheers

The winner of the 2002 Prize in Physics went to Arnd Leike of Ludwig Maximillian University in Munich for mathematically explaining the decay of beer foam over time.

2004 – Five-Second Rule

The 2004 winner in Public Health, high school student Jillian Clarke, asked a question pondered by food eaters everywhere: is the five-second rule a real thing? Do you have five seconds to pick up food that's been dropped on the floor before it becomes polluted with bacteria? The short answer is no. Clarke found that, on ceramic tile surfaces that had been artificially contaminated with E. coli, bacteria transferred onto the food in five seconds or less. Clarke also found that bacteria transfers onto food more quickly from smooth surfaces than rough.

2014 – Slipping Up

In 2014, a team of Japanese physicists – Kiyoshi Mabuchi, Kensei Tanaka, Daichi Uchijima and Rina Sakai – addressed a question that has plagued cartoon-viewers for decades: can you actually slip and fall on a banana skin? To answer this, the physicists measured the friction created between a human shoe, banana peel, and linoleum. They found that a banana skin produces less friction between the shoe and the floor than another similar object. In other words, the banana skin creates a slipping hazard. They attribute the added lubrication to the skin's 'follicular gel'. This research won the 2014 Prize in Physics.

2021 – Cat Talk

The 2021 Prize in Biology went to Swedish scientists Susanne Schötz, Robert Eklund and Joost van de Weijer for analysing the modes of cat-human communication. Over a period of about ten years, these dedicated researchers analysed different sounds produced by cats, such as purring, chirping, chattering, trilling, tweedling, murmuring, meowing, moaning, squeaking, hissing, yowling, howling, growling… (the list goes on). They even tested humans to see how they differentiate between sad meowing (when cats go to the vet) and happy meowing (when cats are about to be fed) simply by listening to recordings of meowing. The results were presented in a scientific paper entitled Melody in Human-Cat Communication (Meowsic): Origins, Past, Present and Future. And yes! Cat lovers were right all along. You can indeed understand your cat… maybe not perfectly, but it turns out that humans can differentiate between sad and happy meowing.

Conundrum C

Why does a mirror reflect an image with left/right reversal, but not top/bottom?

THIS BLESSED PLOT

The Butt Stops Here

Various surveys have taken place regarding British jokes, particularly on the subject or butt of the gag. In his 1909 essay The Humour of the Public, the English humourist Sir Max Beerbohm surveyed the jokes of the music hall and weekly comic papers. He discovered that many jokes were based around: mothers-in-law, hen-pecked husbands, twins, old maids, Jews, Frenchmen, Germans, Italians, African Americans (but not Russians or other foreigners), fatness, thinness, long hair (worn by a man), baldness, seasickness, stuttering, bad cheese and 'shooting the moon' (a slang expression for leaving a lodging house without paying the bill).

Beerbohm argues that the laughter provoked by the items on his list arises from one of two feelings: delight in suffering, or contempt for the unfamiliar. It is not entirely clear where smelly cheese fits in. Richard Boston, in his book An Anatomy of Laughter (Collins, 1974), suggests that the smell can be linked with various bodily smells, which all kids know are very funny indeed. And where would joking be without foreigners? Some of the very earliest jokes for which there is any evidence are those that the ancient Egyptians told at the expense of the Nubians; a long-suffering people who are still the butt of jokes in Egypt today.

In another UK survey, conducted by the Open University and the British Broadcasting Corporation (BBC) between June 2006 and June 2007, over 400 people entered a joke booth, recording over 600 jokes and anecdotes. Half of the jokers were under twenty years old, and a quarter over fifty. There was a similar number of males and females. The most common butts of jokes, in descending order, were: ethnicity and nationality, sex, sexuality and gender, stupidity, religion, celebrity, ageing (old age especially) and class. Of course, some jokes combine butts, like sexuality and ethnicity, and jokes based on wordplay often don't have a clear butt.

Some older jokes would focus on an entire town or village. The village of Gotham, in Nottinghamshire, was the butt of jokes for over 400 years. The story is that, threatened by a visit from King John (reigning 1199–1216), the villagers decided to feign stupidity to avoid the expense entailed by residence of the court. Royal messengers found them engaged in ridiculous tasks, such as trying to drown an eel, and joining hands around a thornbush to trap a cuckoo. Hence, the King decided to stay elsewhere. During the reign of King Henry VIII, around 1540, a pamphlet was published entitled The Merry Tales of the Mad Men of Gotham by a writer using the pseudonym A.B. of Phisicke Doctor. With subsequent editions, the word 'mad' was changed for 'wise', and the myth of the Wise Men of Gotham was born. Wise is perhaps not the correct word to use… A better description might be 'The clever and cunning men of Gotham'. One of the (not-so-clever) tales follows.

The Men of Gotham Cross a River

Seven men from Gotham were walking in the countryside when they found their path blocked by a wide river. It was very deep, but they had no choice but to wade across. On reaching the other side, one man began counting, to make sure everyone was OK. He looked around him and counted six people. The other men did the same, and each came up with six men. They agreed someone must have drowned, without realising they had not counted themselves.

A stranger passing by, amused by their stupidity, offered a solution: *"All sit around that cowpat and dip your noses into it. The number of holes will tell you how many of you survived."*

The 'wise' men did this and discovered there were seven holes. With cow dung on their noses, they thanked the man, and were mightily relieved they had all made it across.

A Class Apart

The British class system has always provided fertile ground for humour. Although definitions of social class vary and remain controversial, most are influenced by factors of wealth, occupation and education. Until the Life Peerages Act 1958, the Parliament of the United Kingdom was organised on a class basis, with the House of Lords representing the hereditary upper class, and the House of Commons representing everybody else. The British monarch is usually viewed as being at the top of the social class structure.

For the writer George Orwell, England was 'the most class-ridden country under the sun'. The traditional classes – working, middle and upper – are no longer sufficient to contain and explain Britain's long-term preoccupation. One survey offers no fewer than seven categories. The middle classes are arguably the most convoluted and complex ensemble, providing countless opportunities for both inter and intraclass humour.

The curious thing about the British class system is that the contempt is mutual. The upper class condemn the middle class as money-grabbers with no taste or culture, and the working class as unwashed and lazy. The middle class consider the upper class to be amoral and extravagant, and the working class to be vulgar. The working class despise the middle-class because they are prim and prudish, and they have never done 'proper' (i.e. manual) work. At the same time, they scorn the upper class because they are brainless, chinless, and exploit the workers. At this point, I thoroughly recommend a television sketch known as The Class Sketch or I Know My Place, featuring John Cleese, Ronnie Barker and Ronnie Corbett, and first broadcast in an episode of David Frost's satirical comedy programme The Frost Report in April 1966 (widely available online).

Without the British class system, a lot of the best humour would be lost. The embodiment of the British classes is found in many classical literary and artistic works, and of course numerous radio and television comedies, which have evolved since the 1950s. In Fawlty Towers, a classic 1970s' situation comedy, every joke is enshrined in class resentment. Basil, a Torquay hotelier, is a mass of lower middle-class insecurities. He is infuriated by the snobbish airs that his coiffured wife Sybil gives herself, and he treats his staff, Polly and Manuel, as if they are enslaved, because they are employees or – in Manuel's case – foreign. Or take The Good Life, another 1970s' sitcom, in which the infinite gradations of the middle class are the backdrop to the humour. Middle-class Margot, one of the main characters, judges the success of her life by its trivia: the shine on her car, the immaculateness of the stripes on her lawn, and the gleam of her crystal sherry decanter. When her neighbours, Tom and Barbara, drop out of the rat race and turn their back garden into an allotment with pigs, Margot is set adrift. She no longer has any yardstick by which to measure her life. The 'Joneses' that she has tried to 'keep up with' are gone.

Dad's Army manages to successfully combine some quintessential aspects of British life into one package: the perils of war, the stiff upper lip, the seaside, and the tension between social classes. The television comedy series, which ran from 1968 to 1977, is set in the south-coast town of Walmington-on-Sea during World War II. Captain George Mainwaring, the local bank manager, appoints himself leader of the town's contingent of Local Defence Volunteers. The pompous Mainwaring has a working-class background but considers himself middle class and looks down on anyone he thinks is beneath him. In a neat reversal of roles and status, the company sergeant, Arthur Wilson, is of upper middle-class stock, serving as a captain in the First World War. Mainwaring's class ambitions frequently lead to conflict with his sergeant. He is left bristling as Wilson recalls his nanny and private school education. The diffident Wilson would invariably undermine Mainwaring's judgement, with a simple and quiet, *"Do you really think that's wise, sir?"*

A Middle Class Connection

The Cambridge Footlights are a world-famous student comedy society who first aired the talents of some of the foremost British comedians and actors. The inaugural performance took place in June 1883 and, in the early days, the Cambridge Footlights amounted to little more than undergraduates, complete with boaters, blazers and white trousers, prancing up and down the stage. The club grew in prominence in the 1960s as a focus of ground-breaking comedy. A leading member was Peter Cook, who went on to launch the satire boom of the sixties, with his Soho club The Establishment, his magazine, Private Eye, and a TV sketch show that outraged the governing classes, That Was the Week That Was. Without the explosion of satire, slapstick and surrealism pioneered by such middle-class performers, British comedy now would be unrecognisable.

At the same time, working-class language burst on to television and transformed the national sense of humour. From one end of the country to the other, laughs came from a couple of Geordie factory electricians in The Likely Lads, and a bickering pair of rag-and-bone men in Steptoe and Son.

The Workers

Steptoe and Son was born of a one-off comic play, The Offer, commissioned by the BBC in 1962 as part of Comedy Playhouse, a series of short plays written by Ray Galton and Alan Simpson. Where previous sitcoms relied on slapstick, gags and farce, Steptoe and Son introduced a note of gritty realism: its characters were resolutely working-class, rag-and-bone men scraping a living by spotting valuables among other people's junk.

Father and son used down-to-earth language and swore like troopers (well, as much as the BBC would allow at that time). Both were made more authentic through being played by 'straight' actors (Wilfred Brambell and Harry H Corbett) rather than comedians. The sitcom's focus was on the inter-generational conflict that characterised the sixties. While father Albert

Steptoe was – as his son often reminded him – a 'dirty old man', entrenched in his grubby and miserly ways, forty-year-old son Harold was filled with social aspirations and pretensions.

Steptoe and Son was a masterclass of comedy and drama. It had an immense influence on British television comedy, and specifically on the writers who created some of the finest British sitcoms of the last fifty years. By the 1980s, working class sitcoms were a staple of the TV landscape.

In 1980, John Sullivan began work on a television series that would become one of the most popular ever screened. Only Fools and Horses tells the story of two bothers trying to rise above their bleak, south London council estate life through various endeavours that ultimately fail. The viewers took an instant liking to the brothers, elevating them to an iconic status in Margaret Thatcher's Britain. Schemer-in-chief Del Boy's regular promise to his loyal but sceptical brother, "*This time next year, we'll be millionaires*" became a national catchphrase. Quite a few sociologists have suggested that their appeal lies in the British love of the underdog.

Till Death Us Do Part also began life as a Comedy Playhouse pilot in 1965, before running for seven series between 1966 and 1975. It became one of the most controversial programmes of its time, and almost certainly would not be commissioned today. The show focuses on the day-to-day lives and opposing opinions of the Garnett family, led by reactionary, white, working-class Alf Garnett, who has racist and anti-socialist views. Alf holds court with his long-suffering wife Else (whom he frequently calls a 'silly moo') his daughter, Rita, and her layabout socialist husband, Mike (referred to as a 'scouse git', and who, in real life, was Prime Minister Tony Blair's father-in-law). The intention of the sitcom was to expose and ridicule Alf's racist views. This was not entirely successful, as his rough and earthy charm actually endeared him to the public. The programme creator, Johnny Speight, observed, "*I didn't create Alf Garnett. Society created him. I just reported him.*"

An Imposing Dowager

The British upper classes have been the centre of many caricatures. One of the finest examples is Lady Augusta Bracknell, who appears in the 1895 comedy play The Importance of Being Ernest. She is one of playwright Oscar Wilde's and, indeed, modern literature's, most preposterous creations. Lady Bracknell is the embodiment of conventional upper-class Victorian respectability. Her ignorant and often absurd comments are a satire of Victorian aristocracy, making her the most quotable of the play's characters. For example:

"The whole theory of modern education is radically unsound. Fortunately, in England at any rate, education produces no effect whatsoever. If it did, it would prove a serious danger to the upper classes, and probably lead to acts of violence in Grosvenor Square."

"I do not approve of anything that tampers with natural ignorance. Ignorance is like a delicate exotic fruit; touch it and the bloom is gone."

"To lose one parent, Mr Worthing, may be regarded as a misfortune; to lose both looks like carelessness."

"Never speak disrespectfully of Society, Algernon. Only people who can't get into it do that."

Upper Class Twits

Dim British aristocrats are invariably the subject of much amusement. The English author and humourist P.G. Wodehouse wrote a series of comic short stories and novels between 1915 and 1974 based on the upper-class nincompoop, Bertie Wooster. On the surface, Bertie is a typical young, upper-class gentleman. He can be described as a man-about-town – a bachelor living with his manservant, Reginald Jeeves, in his flat at Berkeley Mansions in Berkeley Square, London. Bertie is a member of good standing at the Drones Club, a group of privileged 'eggs, beans, and crumpets', educated at select institutions (primarily Eton, Harrow and Oxford). However, Bertie has less awareness of the world than his manservant, who is more intelligent than his master, has a broader vocabulary, and is knowledgeable on English literature, physics, philosophy and psychology. Jeeves is independent, and fully at home with social situations and human interactions. Bertie is helpless without the assistance and advice of Jeeves; sometimes to a point where he resembles a little child who does not know how the world works. This creates the comedy in the stories. Upper-class characters are made to look incompetent and ridiculous, and their servants always save the day. Such characters belong to an English era when permanence and inflexibility in the social order were the norm.

English as Spoken by British People

What the Brits say	What the Brits mean	What others understand
I hear what you say	I disagree and do not want to discuss the matter further	My point of view is accepted
With the greatest respect…	I think you are an idiot	I am being listened to
That's not bad	That's good	That's poor
Quite good	A bit disappointing	Quite good
That is a brave proposal	You are insane	They think I have courage
Very interesting	Clearly nonsense	They are impressed
I'll bear it in mind	I've forgotten it already	They will probably do it
You must come for dinner	It's not an invitation, I'm just being polite	I will get an invitation soon
I have only a few minor comments	Please re-write completely	A few typos have been found
Could we consider some other options	Your idea is unacceptable	They have not yet decided

Royalty

The pinnacle of the upper classes is the British Royal Family. It is unthinkable that King Charles III would be the subject of cruel jokes, but some 200 years ago, satirists would regularly parody the monarch. For example, in 1792, a cartoon by James Gillray depicted King George III and Queen Charlotte seated side-by-side on the lavatory. Both are in the middle of their 'business' – a process accelerated by the entrance of the then Prime Minister, Pitt the Younger, who brings news of the assassination of the King of Sweden.

In the eighteenth century, the monarchy still had, and exercised, power. George III was involved in cabinet appointments – on at least one occasion, he actively brought down a government. He was highly respected, but there was general acceptance that he was also fair game for irreverence and mockery. Gillray's cartoons took aim at the King and Queen again and again. They mocked George's poor eyesight and frugality. They imagined him on the chopping block. In one unpleasant cartoon, Gillray even went so far as to caricature Queen Charlotte naked from the waist up.

George III's son, later George IV, came in for a still harder time. He led an extravagant lifestyle that contributed to the fashions of the Regency era. A notorious ladies' man, George IV has good claim to be the most mercilessly lampooned monarch in British history. And his sex life was fair game. Cartoonists showed him thoroughly enjoying himself under his mistress's skirt, spanking a lady in public, and even having sex with his secret Catholic wife.

These cartoons caused offence – that was the point. But the pictures also attracted much fascination, and were purchased by lords and ladies, members of Parliament, and the royals themselves. Gillray was even granted a government pension – but at this point, the mockery of the monarch did cease. Many of James Gillray's works are held at the National Portrait Gallery in London.

EARTH
CLOSET
ROYAL
LEAK

Conundrum D

John, Paul, George and Ringo don't want to hold each other's hands, so they each stand so that they are exactly two metres from the other three. If you were to draw straight lines from each Beatle to every other Beatle, what shape would be formed?

BREVITY IS THE SOUL OF WIT

Marion's Method

There is a story, certainly apocryphal, about the actor John Wayne during the making of the 1965 film, The Greatest Story Ever Told.

John, playing a Roman centurion, is a witness to the crucifixion of Christ. He had to deliver the line, *"Truly this man was the Son of God."*

In the first take, the line came out rather flatly, so the director, George Stevens, encouraged John to show more emotion, instructing him to *"say it with awe"*.

So he did... on the next take, coming out with, *"Aw, truly this man was the Son of God."*

One-Liners

The early bird might get the worm, but the second mouse gets the cheese.

He who smiles in a crisis has found someone to blame.

If I agreed with you, we'd both be wrong.

A statistician is someone who tells you, when you've got your head in the fridge and your feet in the oven, that you are – on average – very comfortable.

To steal ideas from one person is plagiarism, to steal from many is research.

A Geordie friend of mine advised that when judging Southerners we must always remember that they have not had the benefit of our disadvantages.

If it wasn't for the last minute, nothing would get done.

To err is human, to blame it on someone else shows management potential.

A man can do more than he thinks he can, but he usually does less than he thinks he does.

Artificial intelligence is no match for natural stupidity.

Hard work never killed anyone, but why take the chance?

The trouble with being punctual is that nobody's there to appreciate it.

Nothing is fool proof to a sufficiently talented fool.

If something is sent by ship then it's a cargo, but if it's sent by road then it's a shipment.

There are 10 kinds of people in this world… those who understand binary, and those who don't.

Like so many Americans, she was trying to construct a life that made sense from things she found in gift shops.
Kurt Vonnegut, Jr.

Two-Liners

I asked God for a bicycle, but I know God doesn't work that way. So I stole the bike and asked for forgiveness.
Emo Philips

I said to the gym teacher, *"Can you teach me to do the splits?"* He said, *"How flexible are you?"* I said, *"I can't make Tuesdays."*
Tommy Cooper

Someone complimented me on my driving today. They left a note on the windscreen – it said, 'Parking Fine'.
Tim Vine

Analysing comedy is like dissecting a frog. Nobody laughs and the frog dies.
Barry Cryer

It was only after reading Robert Mugabe's obituary that I realised he came from a small village in Yorkshire. (I suppose it all makes sense if you read his surname backwards.)

I had a job selling hearing aids door to door. It wasn't easy, because your best prospects never answered.
Bob Monkhouse

You can never lose a homing pigeon. If your homing pigeon doesn't come home, then all you have lost is a pigeon.

I once went to one of those parties where everyone throws their car keys into the middle of the room. I don't know who got my moped, but I've been driving that Peugeot for years.
Victoria Wood

Some say, *"If you can't beat them, join them."* I say, *"If you can't beat them, beat them,"* because they will be expecting you to join them, so you will have the element of surprise.

A man walks into a library and asks the librarian for books about paranoia. She whispers, *"They're right behind you!"*

What's the best thing about Switzerland? *"I don't know, but the flag is a big plus."*

And the Lord said to John, *"Come forth and you will receive eternal life."*
But John came fifth and won a toaster.

There are various ways to give up smoking: nicotine patches, nicotine gum. My auntie used to pour a gallon of petrol over herself every morning.
Paul Merton

I saw this advert in a window that said: 'Television for sale, £1, volume stuck on full.' I thought, I can't turn that down.
Tim Vine

Random Thoughts

"The scientists of today think deeply instead of clearly. One must be sane to think clearly, but one can think deeply and be quite insane."
Nikola Tesla

"The aim of a joke is not to degrade the human being, but to remind him that he is already degraded."
George Orwell

"My formula for success is rise early, work late, and strike oil."
J. P. Getty

"Sir, you have tasted two whole worms; you have hissed all my mystery lectures and you have been caught fighting a liar in the quad; you will leave Oxford by the next town drain."
Reverend W. A. Spooner (addressed to an undergraduate)

Nancy Astor: *"If I were your wife, I would put poison in your coffee!"*
Winston Churchill: *"And if I were your husband, I would drink it."*

"Only two things are infinite, the universe and human stupidity, and I'm not sure about the former."
Albert Einstein

"The opposite of a correct statement is a false statement. The opposite of a profound truth may well be another profound truth."
Niels Bohr

"University politics are vicious precisely because the stakes are so small."
Henry Kissinger

"Few things are harder to put up with than a good example."
Mark Twain

"A consensus means that everyone agrees to say collectively what no one believes individually."
Abba Eban

"He is the very pineapple of politeness!"
Mrs Malaprop (in Sheridan's The Rivals)

Small Talk

Lewis Carroll, Alice's Adventures in Wonderland, 1865

"Begin at the beginning," the King said, very gravely, *"and go on till you come to the end: then stop."*

Mad Hatter: *"Why is a raven like a writing-desk?"*
"Have you guessed the riddle yet?" the Hatter said, turning to Alice again.
"No, I give it up," Alice replied: *"What's the answer?"*
"I haven't the slightest idea," said the Hatter.

"Take some more tea," the March Hare said to Alice, very earnestly.
"I've had nothing yet," Alice replied in an offended tone, *"so I can't take more."*
"You mean you can't take less," said the Hatter: *"it's very easy to take more than nothing."*

"Would you tell me, please, which way I ought to go from here?"
"That depends a good deal on where you want to get to," said the Cat.
"I don't much care where – " said Alice.
"Then it doesn't matter which way you go," said the Cat.
"– so long as I get somewhere," Alice added as an explanation.
"Oh, you're sure to do that," said the Cat, *"if you only walk long enough."*

25

Another Friday Night

A man with authority walks into a pub. He orders everyone around.

A ghost walks into a pub. The landlord says, *"Sorry, we don't serve spirits."*

Bill Gates walks into a pub and everyone becomes a billionaire – on average.

Jimmy Wales* walks into a pub…
[*citation needed]

A robot walks into a pub, and the landlord says, *"We don't serve robots."*
The robot replies, *"Someday you will."*

$f(x)$ walks into a pub, and the landlord says, *"Sorry, we don't cater for functions."*
$f'(x)$ walks into a pub, and the landlord says, *"Sorry, we don't cater for functions."*
But that's the same joke!
No, it's derivative humour.

Three logicians walk into a pub. The landlord asks, *"Do all of you want a drink?"*
The first logician says, *"I don't know."*
The second logician says, *"I don't know."*
Finally, the third logician says, *"Yes!"*

A string and his friends walk into a pub, and the string goes up to get a drink. The landlord says, *"We don't serve strings here."* So the string ties himself in a loop, does up the top of his head, and then goes up to the bar, and the landlord says, *"What... are you still a string?"*
And the string replies, *"No, I'm a frayed knot."*

The Door

For Those Who Prefer a Bar

A scalar walks into a bar – and becomes a vector.

A neutrino walks through the bar.

A 100 kilopascals go into a bar.

A woodpecker walks into a bar and says, *"Is the bar tender here?"*

A dyslexic man walks into a bra.

A woman walks into a bar and asks the bartender for a double entendre, so he gives it to her.

The past, present, and future walk into a bar… It was tense.

A weasel walks into a bar. The bartender says, *"Wow, I've never served a weasel before. What can I get you?"*
"Pop," goes the weasel.

Conundrum E

If a = 3, b = 5, c = 0, d = 2, e = 4 and f = 1, what is the value of g?

AND THEREBY HANGS A TALE

Tools of the Job

Parody and satire are popular conduits used by writers and performers for their humour. A parody imitates another work with ridicule or irony, although it may end up a poor version of the original. On the other hand, satire goes a step further and offers commentary and criticism about wider issues in society. The wit can range from the absurdity and nonsense of Catch-22 to the dark ('jokeless') humour found in Slaughterhouse-Five.

Tilting at Windmills

The exploits of Don Quixote and his faithful squire, Sancho Panza, have captured readers' imaginations for 400 years. The novel Don Quixote, originally conceived as a parody of the chivalric romances that had long been popular, was published in two parts (1605 and 1615) by Spanish writer Miguel de Cervantes. Inspired by his readings, an ageing minor nobleman named Alonso Quixano sets out from his home village of La Mancha in pursuit of adventure. Adopting the name Don Quixote, he recruits a simple farmer,

Sancho Panza, to be his squire, promising him an island to govern at the completion of their journeys.

Sancho Panza is the original 'sidekick'; a symbol of practicality over idealism. Throughout their journeys, Sancho plays the straight man to Don Quixote, doing the best he can to correct his master's eccentric fantasies. In one famous scene, our eponymous hero imagines himself fighting giants when he attacks windmills.

Just then they came in sight of thirty or forty windmills that rise from that plain. And no sooner did Don Quixote see them that he said to his squire, *"Fortune is guiding our affairs better than we ourselves could have wished. Do you see over yonder, friend Sancho, thirty or forty hulking giants? I intend to do battle with them and slay them. With their spoils we shall begin to be rich for this is a righteous war and the removal of so foul a brood from the face of the earth is a service God will bless."*

"What giants?" asked Sancho Panza.

Don Quixote is tall and thin, Sancho is short and fat. The mismatched couple remains an archetypal literary comedy duo. Sancho is an illiterate commoner and provides comments throughout the novel with proverbs, known as sanchismos, which are a combination of broad humour and earthy wit.

"There's a remedy for everything except death."

"The lucky man has nothing to worry about."

"The foolish remarks of the rich man pass for wisdom in the world."

"Make yourself into honey and the flies will eat you up."

"You're worth as much as you have."

"You can't take vengeance on the landed gentry."

"If the pitcher hits the stone or the stone hits the pitcher, it's bad for the pitcher."

"The fool knows more in his own house than the wise man in someone else's."

While Don Quixote is a comic work, the novel's message that individuals can be right while society is wrong was considered radical for its day.

Big-Endians and Little-Endians

Gulliver's Travels is a four-part satirical work by Anglo-Irish author Jonathan Swift, published anonymously in 1726 as Travels into Several Remote Nations of the World. A parody of the then popular travel narrative, Gulliver's Travels combines adventure with savage satire, mocking English customs and the politics of the day.

Two countries visited by Gulliver are Lilliput and Blefuscu. These were intended as depictions of the Kingdoms of Great Britain and France, respectively. Only the internal politics of Lilliput are described in detail; these are spoofs of British politics, in which the great issues of the day are demeaned and become trivialities.

The two major political parties were the Whigs and the Tories. The Tories are parodied as the Tramecksan or 'High-Heels' (due to their adhesion to the high-church policy of the Church of England, and their exalted views of royal supremacy), while the Whigs are represented as the Slamecksan or 'Low-Heels' (the Whigs inclined towards low-church views, believed in parliamentary supremacy, and were more liberal). These issues, generally considered to be of fundamental importance to the constitution of Great Britain, are reduced by Swift to a difference in shoe fashions. The Emperor of Lilliput is described as a devotee of the Low-Heels, just as King George I employed only Whigs in his administration. The Emperor's heir is described as having 'one of his heels higher than the other', which denotes the support by the Prince of Wales (the future George II) of the political opposition during his father's life. As a Lilliputian, the Prince wobbles when he walks.

The novel further describes an intra-Lilliputian quarrel over the practice of breaking eggs. Traditionally, Lilliputians broke boiled eggs at the larger end; a few generations ago, an Emperor of Lilliput, the present Emperor's great-grandfather, had decreed that all eggs be broken at the smaller end after his son cut himself breaking the egg at the larger end. The differences between Big-Endians (those who broke their eggs at the larger end) and Little-Endians had given rise to 'six rebellions... wherein one Emperor lost his life, and another his crown'. The Lilliputian religion says an egg should be broken at the convenient end, which is now interpreted by the Lilliputians as the smaller end. The Big-Endians gained favour in Blefuscu.

The Big-Endian/Little-Endian controversy reflects, in a much-simplified form, British disputes over religion. Less than 200 years before, England had been a Catholic (Big-Endian) country; but a series of reforms beginning in the 1530s under King Henry VIII, Edward VI and Queen Elizabeth I had converted most of the country to Protestantism (Little-Endianism), in the form of the Church of England.

Swift also had something to say about science and technology. He mocked the assumption that scientific revolution had transformed European culture for the better. In a visit to the city of Lagado, Gulliver stumbles upon the 'Grand Academy', and describes pointless experiments to extract sunbeams from cucumbers and to build houses from the roof downwards. The Academy of Lagado also provides a scientific approach to reconciling the violently opposing views of some senators. Their brains would be cut in half and interchanged, with opposing halves joined in the head of one senator. In this way, political debate would be confined within one skull, which would lead to a rapid compromise. This gives a new meaning to the idiom 'banging heads together'.

More Equal Than Others

In 1945, the English journalist and novelist George Orwell published a political fable based on the events of Russia's Bolshevik Revolution of 1917 and the betrayal of the cause by Joseph Stalin. Animal Farm describes a group of animals who overthrow their exploitative human masters to set up an egalitarian society of their own.

Mr Jones, a cruel and drunken farmer, manages Manor Farm. The animals gather one day to hear Old Major, a wise old pig, speak. Old Major urges the animals to revolt against their farmers. A few days later, Old Major passes away, leaving three younger pigs – Snowball, Napoleon and Squealer – to formulate the main principles of a philosophy called 'Animalism'. Late one night, the animals manage to defeat Mr Jones in a battle, running him off the land. The property is renamed Animal Farm, and organised according to seven commandments, the most important of which is 'all animals are equal'. The phrase 'four legs good, two legs bad' becomes a popular sheep song.

The power-loving leaders, the pigs, have opposing views on how Animal Farm should be run. They eventually subvert the revolution, forming a dictatorship that is even more oppressive and heartless than that of their former human masters. The pigs cooperate with people and begin to adopt human characteristics, such as living in the farmhouse and walking on two legs. The sheep are taught a new chant – 'four legs good, two legs better' – while the former commandment is updated to 'all animals are equal, but some animals are more equal than others'.

Orwell wrote Animal Farm between November 1943 and February 1944, when the United Kingdom was in its wartime alliance with the Soviet Union against Nazi Germany, and the British intelligentsia held Stalin in high esteem... something Orwell despised.

4 LEGS GOOD
2 LEGS BAD
4 LEGS GOO
2 LEGS BAD
4 LEGS GOOD
2 LEGS BAD

But There's a Catch

Catch-22, published in 1961 by the American author Joseph Heller, tells the account of a US Army squadron based in Italy during the Second World War. The story centres on John Yossarian, a bombardier with the Army Air Corps. Captain Yossarian is bewildered, seeking to understand why everyone is trying to kill him. Not only do strangers shoot at his plane whenever he drops a bomb, but his senior officials put his life at risk for their own advancement to higher ranks.

Yossarian shares his fears with Clevinger, a highly principled member of the squadron who acts as his foil within the story:

"They're trying to kill me," Yossarian told him calmly.

"No one's trying to kill you," Clevinger cried.

"Then why are they shooting at me?" Yossarian asked.

"They're shooting at everyone," Clevinger answered. *"They're trying to kill everyone."*

"And what difference does that make?"

As Colonel Cathcart keeps increasing the number of missions, Yossarian becomes more and more fearful of losing his life in action. Doc Daneeka, the flight surgeon, is required to ground anyone who is insane. Since no sane man would continue to voluntarily fly such dangerous missions, all Yossarian must do is request that he be relieved of duty. But there's a problem.

"You mean there's a catch?"

"Sure there's a catch," Doc Daneeka replied. *"Catch-22. Anyone who wants to get out of combat duty isn't really crazy."*

A man is considered insane if he willingly continues to fly dangerous combat missions, but if he makes the necessary formal request to be relieved of such missions, the very act of making the request proves that he is sane, and therefore ineligible to be relieved.

There was only the one catch, which added a new term to the dictionary.

So It Goes

Eight years after Catch-22, another acclaimed anti-war satirical work was published. This was Slaughterhouse-Five, a novel by the American author Kurt Vonnegut Jr. It follows the life and experiences of Billy Pilgrim, from his early years to his time as an American soldier and chaplain's assistant during World War II, to the post-war years, with Billy occasionally travelling through time. Whereas Catch-22 is 'crazy funny', seeing war as mad, and the desire to escape combat as the only sane position, Slaughterhouse-Five does not see war as farcical. Vonnegut is a sad-faced comedian and uses black (or gallows) humour. Writing in the New Yorker, Salman Rushdie notes that if Heller was Charlie Chaplin, then Vonnegut was Buster Keaton.

Slaughterhouse-Five rejects conventional story writing, presenting its episodes in a deliberately mixed-up and fragmentary manner. The narrative uses science fiction and introduces the perspective of the inhabitants of the planet Tralfamadore, for whom time is not linear. The phrase 'so it goes' appears after every mention of death and mortality in Slaughterhouse-Five. This seemingly flippant saying reflects a Tralfamadorian philosophy that comforts Billy Pilgrim: while a person is dead at one particular moment, they are still alive and well at all of the other moments of their life, because all time exists at once. There is a link here to the thoughts of some theoretical physicists.

"How – how does the Universe end?" said Billy.

"We blow it up, experimenting with new fuels for our flying saucers. A Tralfamadorian test pilot presses a starter button, and the whole Universe disappears."

So it goes.

The Answer to Life, the Universe and Everything

The Hitchhiker's Guide to the Galaxy, written by English author, screenwriter and dramatist Douglas Adams, began life as a BBC radio comedy in 1978, a year before the first book (adapted from the first four radio episodes) was published. Adams wrote four more volumes before he died, in 2001.

The saga has as its hero a hapless, ordinary Englishman, Arthur Dent, who unexpectedly finds himself adrift in a universe characterised by randomness and absurdity. Arthur, whose house is about to be demolished for a planned road bypass, is lying down in front of a bulldozer when his friend, Ford Prefect (in 1950s' Britain, the Ford Prefect was a popular car) arrives and tells him it is imperative that they go to the pub immediately. There, Ford explains that he is from a small planet near Betelgeuse, and that another alien species, the Vogons, are about to destroy the Earth to make way for a hyperspace express route. Following the destruction of Earth, the plot of The Hitchhiker's Guide centres on a bemused Arthur Dent wandering the Universe with Ford Prefect and a crew of eccentrics, including two-headed galactic President Zaphod Beeblebrox, an unhappy robot named Marvin, and Trillian, an astrophysicist.

Adams pokes fun at religion, science, politics, bureaucracy, climate change, and greed. The Vogons, for instance, are an alien race collectively disinclined to save their grandmothers from certain death without orders 'signed in triplicate, sent in, sent back, queried, lost, found, subjected to public inquiry, lost again, and finally buried in soft peat for three months and recycled as firelighters'. As for politics, Adams notes, 'Anyone capable of getting themselves made President should on no account be allowed to do the job.'

In the radio series and the first novel, a group of hyper-intelligent pan-dimensional beings demand to learn the answer to the ultimate question of life, the universe, and everything from a supercomputer called Deep Thought, specially built for this purpose. After 7.5 million years of calculation, the answer turns out to be 42.

Despite Adams revealing that his choice of 42 was somewhat arbitrary, millions of Hitchhiker's fans still ponder on what they imagine was a secret meaning. Here are some of their thoughts:

- Elvis Presley died at the age of 42.
- Cricket has 42 laws.
- In William Shakespeare's Romeo and Juliet, Friar Laurence gives Juliet a potion that allows her to be in a death-like coma for 'two and forty hours'.
- The result of the most famous game in English football – the World Cup final of 1966 – was 4-2.
- In the Book of Revelation, it is prophesised that the beast will hold dominion over the earth for 42 months.

Conundrum F

Jack is looking at Jill but Jill is looking at George. Jack is married but George is not. Is a married person looking at an unmarried person?

NEITHER A BORROWER NOR A LENDER BE

Time Is Money

Time is money
Money talks
So time talks
But talk is cheap
So time is cheap
But time is money
So money is cheap
Which it's not

Let Them Eat Grass

One afternoon, an estate agent was driving his luxury BMW when he saw two men along the roadside eating grass. Disturbed, he stopped and got out to investigate.

He asked one man, "*Why are you eating grass?*"

"*We don't have any money for food,*" the poor man replied. "*We need to eat grass.*"

"*Well, you can come with me to my house and I'll feed you,*" the estate agent said.

"*But sir, I have a wife and two children with me. They are over there, under that tree.*"

"*Bring them along,*" the estate agent replied. Turning to the other poor man, he stated, "*You can come with us, too.*"

The second man, in a pitiful voice, then said, "*But sir, I also have a wife and SIX children!*"

"*Bring them along as well,*" the estate agent answered.

They all got in the car; no easy task. Once underway, one of the poor fellows turned to the estate agent and said, "*Sir, you are too kind. Thank you for taking all of us with you.*"

The estate agent replied, "*Glad to do it. You'll really love my place. The grass is almost a foot high.*"

Race to the Top

A British university and a Japanese university decided to have a competitive boat race on the River Wear. The Japanese university won by 100 yards. The British university was very dispirited by this result, and staff began to leave.

Senior management had to uncover the reason for this crushing defeat, as it was affecting morale, and so a project team was established to investigate the problem and recommend appropriate action. The outcome of the investigation was:

The Japanese university team had eight people rowing and one person steering. The British university team had one person rowing and eight people steering.

The senior management committee met and, in light of this discovery, immediately hired a consultancy company to review the British university's structure.

After six months and £500,000, their report concluded that too many people were steering and not enough were rowing. To prevent such an embarrassing defeat at the hand of the Japanese in the following year, the senior management committee of the British university completely restructured the rowing team to four 'steering managers', three 'senior steering managers', one 'executive steering manager', and one 'rower'. A performance-related review scheme was introduced as an incentive for the rower to work harder.

The following year, the Japanese boat won by 200 yards.

The British university laid off its rower due to poor performance, sold off all its oars, cancelled its capital investment programme for new equipment, and halted development on the new boat.

It then awarded exceptional performance bonuses to the consultants for identifying the problem and the senior management for the cost savings by abandoning the competition.

Thank goodness this is only a fairy story and couldn't happen in real life!

The Ways of Business

Dad: *"Son, I want you to marry a girl of my choice."*

Son: *"No."*

Dad: *"The girl is Bill Gates' daughter."*

Son: *"Okay then."*

Dad goes to Bill Gates.

Dad: *"I want your daughter to marry my son."*

Bill Gates: *"No."*

Dad: *"My son is the CEO of the world's greatest bank."*

Bill Gates: *"Okay then."*

Dad goes to the chairman of the world's greatest bank.

Dad: *"Make my son the CEO."*

Chairman: *"No."*

Dad: *"My son is the son-in-law of Bill Gates."*

Chairman: *"Okay then."*

This is business.

My Financial Career

Stephen Leacock, 1910 (Professor Leacock was an English-born Canadian teacher, political scientist and writer. During the early 1900s, he was the most famous humourist writing in the English language. At one point, it was said that more people had heard of Stephen Leacock than had heard of Canada. Here, he describes the anguish he experienced on opening a bank account. I have updated the text somewhat to modern parlance.)

When I go into a bank, I get anxious. The clerks frighten me; the grills at the counter frighten me; the sight of the money frightens me; everything frightens me. The moment I cross the threshold of a bank and attempt to transact business there, I become an irresponsible idiot.

I knew this beforehand, but my salary had been raised to fifty dollars a month and I felt that the bank was the only place for it. So I shambled in and looked timidly around at the clerks. I had the thought that a person about to open an account must consult the manager. I went up to a grill marked 'Accountant'. The accountant was a tall, cool devil. The very sight of him frightened me. My voice was sepulchral.

"Can I see the manager?" I said, and added solemnly, *"Alone."* I don't know why I said 'alone'.

"Certainly," said the accountant, and fetched him.

The manager was a grave, calm man. I clutched my fifty-six dollars in a crumpled ball in my pocket.

"Are you the manager?" I said. God knows I didn't doubt it.

"Yes," he said.

"Can I see you," I asked, *"alone?"* I didn't want to say 'alone' again but thought that the situation necessitated it.

The manager looked at me with some alarm. He felt that I had an awful secret to reveal.

"Come in here," he said, and led the way to a private room. He turned the key

in the lock.

"We are safe from interruption here," he said; *"sit down."*

We both sat down and looked at each other. I found no voice to speak.

"You are one of Pinkerton's men, I presume," he said. He had gathered from my mysterious manner that I was a detective. I knew what he was thinking, and it made things worse.

"No, not Pinkerton," I said, seeming to imply that I came from a rival agency.

"To tell the truth," I went on, as if I had been prompted to lie about it, *"I am not a detective at all. I have come to open an account. I intend to keep all my money in this bank."*

The manager looked relieved but still serious; he concluded now that I was a son of Baron Rothschild.

"A large account, I suppose," he said.

"Fairly large," I whispered. *"I propose to deposit fifty-six dollars now and fifty dollars a month regularly."*

The manager got up and opened the door. He called to the accountant.

"Mr Montgomery," he said, unkindly loudly, *"this gentleman is opening an account. He will deposit fifty-six dollars. Good morning."*

I rose. A big iron door stood open at the side of the room. *"Good morning,"* I said, and stepped into the safe.

"Come out," said the manager coldly, and showed me the other way. I went up to the accountant's counter and poked the ball of money at him with a quick convulsive movement, as if I were doing a conjuring trick. My face was ghastly pale.

"Here," I said, *"deposit it."* The tone of the words seemed to mean, *"Let us do this painful thing while the mood is right."* He took the money and gave it to another clerk. He made me write the sum on a slip and sign my name in a book. I no longer knew what I was doing. The bank swam before my eyes.

"Is it deposited?" I asked in a hollow, vibrating voice.

"*It is,*" said the accountant.

"*Then I want to draw a cheque.*"

My idea was to draw out six dollars for present use. Someone gave me a chequebook through a grill and someone else began telling me how to write it out. The people in the bank had the impression that I was an invalid millionaire. I wrote something on the cheque and thrust it in at the clerk. He looked at it.

"*What! Are you taking it all out again?*" he asked in surprise. Then I realised that I had written fifty-six instead of six. I was too far gone to reason, now. I had a feeling that was impossible to explain. All the clerks had stopped writing to look at me. Reckless with misery, I made the plunge.

"*Yes, the whole thing.*"

"*You want to withdraw all your money from the bank?*"

"*Every cent of it.*"

"*Are you not going to deposit any more?*" said the clerk, astonished.

"*Never.*" A remote hope occurred to me that they might think something had insulted me while I was writing the cheque and that I had changed my mind. I made a wretched attempt to look like a man with a fearfully quick temper.

The clerk prepared to pay the money.

"*How will you have it?*" he said.

"*What?*"

"*How will you have it?*"

"*Oh*" – I caught his meaning and answered without even trying to think – "*in fifties.*"

He gave me a fifty-dollar bill.

"*And the six?*" he asked dryly.

"*In sixes,*" I said.

He gave it to me and I rushed out.

As the big door swung behind me, I caught the echo of a roar of laughter that went up to the ceiling of the bank.

Since then, I bank no more. I keep my money in cash in my trouser pocket and my savings in silver dollars in a sock.

Reverse-Charge Call

"Hello, Reverend Lovejoy? This is the Inland Revenue. Do you know a Mr James Morris?"

"I do."

"Is he a member of your congregation?"

"He is."

"Did he donate £50,000 to your church?"

"He will."

Ill-Gotten Gains

A young, inexperienced bank robber gets caught during his first job and ends up in court. Crucial evidence – including video camera footage from the bank's lobby – has gone astray. After weeks of deliberation, conflicting witness statements, a hung jury and considerable frustration, the young man is found not guilty.

As the foreman delivers the verdict, the defendant pipes up, *"Does that mean I can keep the money?"*

Ask an Expert?

A police officer arrives at the scene of an accident to find a car smashed into a tree. The officer rushes over to the vehicle and asks the driver, *"Are you seriously hurt?"*

"How should I know?" the driver responds. *"I'm not a lawyer!"*

Back to Basics

An American businessman was on holiday in a small coastal village in Cornwall. Walking by the harbour one day, he noticed a small boat mooring, with just one fisherman. Inside the boat were several large yellowfin tuna. The American complimented the fisherman on the quality of his fish and asked how long it took to catch them. The fisherman replied that it only took a little while. The businessman then asked why he didn't stay out longer and catch more fish. The fisherman said he had enough to support his family's immediate needs.

The American then asked, *"But what do you do with the rest of your time?"*

The fisherman replied, *"I sleep late, fish a little, play with my children, tend my garden, walk with my wife on the coastal path, and stroll into the village each evening where I have a pint or two in my local pub, and then play darts with my mates. I have a full and busy life."*

The American scoffed. *"I am a Harvard MBA and could help you. You should spend more time fishing, and with the proceeds, buy a bigger boat. With the profit from the bigger boat, you could then buy several boats. Eventually you would have a fleet of fishing boats. Instead of selling your catch to a middleman, you would sell directly to the processor, eventually opening your own cannery. You would control the product, processing, and distribution. You would need to leave this small coastal fishing village and move to London, or even New York, where you would run your expanding enterprise."*

The fisherman asked, *"But how long will this all take?"*

To which the American replied, "*Fifteen or twenty years.*"

"*And then what?*"

The American laughed and said, "*That's the best part. When the time is right, you would float your company on the Stock Exchange and become very rich. You would make millions.*"

"*Millions? What then?*"

The businessman replied, "*Then you would retire. Move to a small coastal fishing village where you would sleep late, play with your grandchildren, spend time gardening, walk with your wife, and stroll into the village in the evenings, where you could drink beer and play darts with your friends.*"

Public Relations

Passenger: "*Is this my train?*"

Station Master: "*No, it belongs to the railway company.*"

Passenger: "*Don't try to be funny. I mean to ask if I can take this train to Durham.*"

Station Master: "*No Madam, I'm afraid it's far too heavy.*"

Conundrum G

Arrange six glasses in a row. Looking from left to right, the first three are filled with water and the other three are empty. By only moving one glass, can you arrange the glasses so that they alternate full and empty?

ALL THE WORLD'S A STAGE

Many a True Word Is Spoken in Jest

Throughout history, in all kinds of society, there have been individuals whose role is to be the focus of laughter, but who have an influence far beyond humour. In folklore and mythology, the figure of a clown or fool takes many forms, the most common of which is the trickster. This is a character who may be a practical joker, a troublemaker, and a source of laughter. The trickster invariably exhibits a considerable intellect or secret knowledge and uses this to play tricks or otherwise disobey normal rules, and defy conventional behaviour. In Greek mythology, the trickster takes the form of Hermes, the son of Zeus, and a messenger. He can move quickly and freely between the worlds of the mortal and the divine, aided by his winged sandals. The equivalent trickster in Roman mythology is Mercury.

The Beatles' song The Fool on the Hill is about a solitary figure who is not understood by others, but whose foolish behaviour belies wisdom. In his authorised biography, Many Years from Now (Secker & Warburg, 1997), Paul McCartney says he first got the idea for the song from the Dutch design collective The Fool, who were the Beatles' favourite designers in 1967. They told him that they had derived their identity from the Tarot card of the same name.

A jester, court jester, or fool was a member of the household of a nobleman or monarch employed to entertain guests during the medieval and Renaissance eras in England. Another link to playing cards is suggested by Richard Boston. In his book An Anatomy of Laughter (Collins, 1974), he notes that the position of the court jester is like that of the joker in a deck of cards. Not only is he not part of the royal family (having no suit), he is also not even properly part of the pack. At the same time, he is the most powerful card in the deck. The joker is at once everything and nothing.

Medieval jesters held privileges that were not afforded to many other persons at court. He (or she – there were females appointed to this role) was one of the few characters in the court who could freely speak their mind without causing offence, and somebody who could use humour to mock, jibe and joke at the expense of the nobles of the court. Jesters came from a wide variety of backgrounds, and many of them were well educated. The court jester is a universal phenomenon and crops up in every court in Europe, China, India, Japan, Russia, America and Africa.

Henry VIII of England employed a jester named Will Sommers; his daughter Mary was entertained by Jane Foole. Thomas Cromwell appreciated that Sommers sometimes drew the King's attention to extravagance and waste within the royal household by means of a joke. Queen Elizabeth I rebuked a fool called Clod for not criticising her more severely. There are other stories that show a jester as the only person who could counsel a stubborn king, and as such, the myth of the court jester suggests that they could act as a check on the whimsical power of absolute monarchy. My own favourite royal jester must be Roland the Farter, a medieval flautist who lived in the twelfth century and was the fool of Henry II. He was best known for one thing and one thing alone.

Shakespeare wrote many fools into his plays, most of whom were treated respectfully. These include Touchstone (As You Like It), Feste (Twelfth Night), Trinculo (The Tempest) and (the) Fool (King Lear). In a very famous speech, Hamlet addresses the skull of Yorick, his father's jester, fondly remembering his childhood and reflecting on the fleeting nature of human life.

The fool is most important in an authoritarian society. His nothingness is complementary to a monarch's sovereignty. When kings lose their power, the importance of fools is diminished. After the Restoration in 1660, Charles II did not reinstate the tradition of the court jester. Across the channel, the office died out with the French Revolution. However, there have been a few attempts to bring back the tradition. In 2004, English Heritage appointed Nigel Roder ('Kester the Jester') as the State Jester for England, the first since Muckle John, who lost his job – but kept his head – when his boss, Charles I, was executed. However, following an objection by the National Guild of Jesters, English Heritage accepted that they were not authorised to grant such a title. Roder was succeeded as 'Heritage Jester' by Pete Cooper ('Peterkin the Fool'). And in 2015, the town of Conwy in North Wales appointed Russel Erwood ('Erwyd le Fol') as the official resident jester of the town and its people; a post that had been vacant since 1295.

Life After Death

As told by Billy Connolly on The Michael Parkinson Show in 1975; a joke that propelled Billy to stardom

A conversation is occurring between two Glaswegians.

I says, *"How's the wife?"*

He says, *"Aw she's deed."*

"Whit?"

"Deed, out the game. Deed. I murdered her. I'll show you if you want."

I says, *"Aye, show me."*

So we go away up to his tenement building out the close – that's the entrance to the tenement – and sure enough there's a big mound of earth, but there's a bum sticking out of it.

I says, *"Is that her?"* and he says, *"Aye."*

I says, *"What did you leave her bum sticking out for?"*

He says, *"I need somewhere to park my bike."*

BIKE PARK

Misunderstandings, Mystification and Misdirection

Many professions have developed their own vocabulary; in most cases, to ensure easy communication between colleagues, but in some instances, to confuse other professions and bamboozle members of the public. Scientists, doctors, dentists, and accountants are notorious for this; using language that abounds in jargon and acronyms. Solicitors bewilder their clients by keeping to simple wording in their documents but removing all the punctuation. Estate agents communicate in a dialect renowned for its convoluted syntax and peculiar vocabulary, walking the tightrope between salesmanship and fraudulence. All too familiar to the exhausted house hunter are the euphemisms 'compact', 'bijou', 'cosy', 'ample storage', 'conveniently located', 'low-maintenance garden' and (always) 'viewing recommended'.

In a world apart, we have our politicians, who not only have their own words, but almost a new language. George Orwell recognised what was happening and did some extrapolation. 'Newspeak' is the fictional language of Oceania, a superstate that is the setting of his dystopian novel Nineteen Eighty-Four. In the novel, the ruling English Socialist Party, Ingsoc, create Newspeak to meet the ideological requirements of English Socialism in Oceania.

Newspeak is a controlled language of simplified grammar and restricted vocabulary designed to limit the individual's ability to think and articulate 'subversive' concepts such as personal identity, self-expression and free will. These are criminalised as 'thoughtcrime' since they contradict the prevailing Ingsoc orthodoxy. We are some way from this totalitarian future (it might be argued that there are worrying trends) but everyone will recognise the words and phrases that are much loved by our politicians.

Here is some insight into the thinking of our politicians, with extracts taken from 'The Politicians' Speechmaking Guidebook'.

I'm sorry, but...
Use if you mean to say 'I'm not sorry, and...'

Ideological
Someone with fixed ideas whom we dislike. If we do like them, try 'committed'.

Misguided
Their intentions are good, but they are idiots.

Too little, too late
Use to describe the quality of our opponents' proposals when they are in serious danger of being popular.

We must focus on the immediate issue
And not the thing you keep asking about (an excellent phrase for deflecting a question).

We need to look more widely
… until we find some evidence that supports our conclusions.

We rule nothing out
We are ruling lots of things out, including the thing you just said, but this isn't the moment to tell you.

Worrying
The nature of a report that makes no specific criticisms. If it is a long report, try 'extremely worrying'. If it really is worrying, the word 'disturbing' is more appropriate.

Let me be very clear
A very useful phase that can be inserted at the beginning of answers when these are likely to be somewhat vague.

Levelling up
Get this into speeches as often as possible when visiting the north of the UK as it suggests we are doing something significant to help the area.

Sacrifice

Elton John is dining out one night when a young man comes up to his table.

"Mr John," says the lad, *"my name is Bentley Drummle. Could you please do me a favour?"*

"What kind of favour?" Elton asks.

"Well, I'm here with my girlfriend and I want to make a good impression on her. I certainly would appreciate it if you would drop by my table and say 'Hi, Bentley'."

"OK, I'll try," says the singer, smiling. A little later, he approaches the lad's table, and says, *"Hi, Bentley!"*

The young man looks up at him and snaps, *"Not now, Elton. Can't you see I'm busy?"*

Cowisms

'-ism' is a suffix added to the end of many English words, originally derived from the Ancient Greek. It means 'taking side with' or 'imitation of', and is often used to describe philosophies, theories, religions, social movements and behaviours. By the nineteenth century it was being used by Thomas Carlyle to suggest a pre-packaged ideology. Today, the suffix is invariably applied to signify political or religious movements.

The following definitions circulated throughout the United States in the mid-1930s under the title Parable of the Isms.

SOCIALISM:
You have two cows. The State takes one and gives it to someone else.

COMMUNISM:
You have two cows. The State takes both and gives you the milk it thinks you need.

FASCISM:
You have two cows. The State takes both and sells you the milk.

CAPITALISM:
You have two cows. You sell one and buy a bull. Your herd multiplies, and the economy grows. You sell them and retire on the income.

NATIONAL SOCIALISM (NAZISM):
You have two cows. The State takes both and shoots you.

And some more recent isms.

VENTURE CAPITALISM:
You have two cows. You sell three of them to your publicly listed company, using letters of credit opened by your brother-in-law at the bank, and then execute a debt/equity swap with an associated general offer so that you get all four cows back, with a tax exemption for five cows. The milk rights of the six cows are transferred via an intermediary to a Cayman Island company secretly owned by the majority shareholder, who sells the rights to all seven cows back to your listed company. The annual report says the company owns eight cows, with an option on one more.

ENVIRONMENTALISM:
You have two cows. The government bans you from milking or killing them.

Get to the Point

A Roman senator comes into the Senate fifteen minutes late one day. Cicero is making a speech, so he quietly takes his seat and whispers to the senator next to him, "*What's he talking about?*" The senator replies, "*I don't know, he hasn't got to the verb.*"

Tears of a Clown

A man walks into a psychiatrist's office.

"Doctor, I just don't think I can go on. Life has no meaning for me. Everywhere I see nothing but misery and sadness."

The psychiatrist replies,

"What you need is to cheer up and learn to laugh. I know just the thing – the greatest clown in Europe is performing with the circus this week. His name is Grock. See him and you'll be sure to forget your troubles."

The man shakes his head.

"Doctor," he replies, "I am Grock."

Conundrum H

The UK public elects 650 members of Parliament to represent their interests and concerns in the House of Commons. Suppose the same number of people vote in each of the UK's 650 constituencies, and four candidates stand in each seat. To the nearest whole number:

1. What is the lowest possible percentage of the national vote that could give one party an overall majority of 326 seats?
2. What is the highest possible percentage that a party could obtain and NOT secure an overall majority?

NEITHER RHYME NOR REASON

The Famous Eccles

Spike Milligan (1918-2002) was one of the most influential humourists of the twentieth century. His work, particularly as one of the legendary Goons (alongside Peter Sellers, Harry Secombe and Michael Bentine) in the 1950s' BBC radio hit The Goon Show, changed the face of British comedy. The surreal humour and Spike's anarchic sense of absurdity made him a model for succeeding generations of comedians and paved the way for the Monty Python brand of alternative comedy.

One of Milligan's creations in the Goons was Eccles, a complete and utter idiot. 'The Famous Eccles' (as he referred to himself) was an amiable, well-meaning man with no intellect or understanding. His idiotic logic typifies Goon humour.

In a conversation with Bluebottle, a young boy scout with a squeaky voice, who gets blown up in each episode (and played by Peter Sellers):

Bluebottle: *"What time is it, Eccles?"*

Eccles: *"Err, just a minute. I, I've got it written down 'ere on a piece of paper. A nice man wrote the time down for me this morning."*

In 2000, Spike famously described Prince Charles – a long-time fan – as *"a little grovelling bastard"* on live television. He followed this up with a fax to the Prince, commenting: *"I suppose a knighthood is out of the question?"* In fact, in the New Year Honours list of 2001, Spike was made an honorary knight ('honorary' because he was an Irish citizen).

Spike Milligan once quipped that he wanted the headstone on his grave to bear the inscription 'I told you I was ill'. The Diocese of Chichester refused to allow this epitaph, but a compromise was reached to include the Irish translation of the words.

Obliteration by Onomatopoeia

Jimmy Carr

A cowboy walks into a bar and orders a whisky.

As the barman's pouring it, the cowboy looks around him.

"Where is everyone?" he says.

"Gone to the hanging," says the barman.

"Hanging?" says the cowboy. *"Who are they hanging?"*

"Brownpaper Pete," replies the barman.

"Brownpaper Pete? Why do they call him that?"

"Well," says the barman. *"His hat's made of brown paper, his shirt's made of brown paper, his jacket's made of brown paper and his trousers are made of*

brown paper."

"Really?" says the cowboy. *"What are they hanging him for?"*

"Rustling."

Divine Revelation?

A man falls into a deep well, but near the bottom, he grabs a tree root, which stops his fall. He cannot hold on much longer and cries out, *"Is there anyone up there?"*

A beam of light shines down on him and a deep voice says, *"I, the Lord, am here. Let go of the root and I will help you."*

The man then shouts, *"Is there anyone else up there?"*

Seeing the Light

Jimmy Carr

Two old Jewish men were strolling down the street one day when they happened to walk past a Catholic church. Above the door of the church they saw a large sign that said, 'Convert to Catholicism and get £25'. One of the Jewish men stopped walking and stared at the sign. The other turned to his friend and said, *"Murray, what's going on?"*

"Abe," replied Murray, *"I'm thinking of doing it."*

With that, Murray strode purposefully into the church.

Twenty minutes later, he came out with his head bowed.

'So," asked Abe, *"did you get the twenty-five pounds?"*

Murray looked up at him and snapped, *"Is that all you people think about?"*

As Told to the Bishop of Leeds

The Bishop of Leeds revealed that during a telephone conversation with Barry Cryer, he asked if Barry had any decent jokes he could use at Christmas.

Here is Barry's gag.

A man and his wife are out walking one day when they spot a bloke sitting alone in a bus shelter on the other side of the road.

"*That looks like the Archbishop of Canterbury over there,*" says the woman. "*Go and ask him if he is.*"

The husband crosses the road and asks the man if he is indeed the Archbishop of Canterbury.

"*Fuck off,*" says the man.

The husband crosses back to his wife, who asks: "*What did he say? Is he the Archbishop of Canterbury?*"

"*He told me to fuck off,*" says the husband.

"*Oh no,*" replies the wife, "*now we'll never know.*"

SUPERMARKET
BUS STOP
Canterbury
ALDI

Holiday Memoirs

On a recent nine-day holiday with friends, we went out to a local restaurant for the first eight nights for a meal. On the ninth evening we went to a local cinema to watch The Dark Knight.

It was a memorable time:

'Dinner, dinner, dinner, dinner;

dinner, dinner, dinner, dinner;

Batman.'

Seeing Red

Two men are driving through Gateshead when they come up to a red light. The driver puts his foot down hard on the accelerator and they go zooming past the red light.

His friend looks at him and says, *"Hey, you just went through a red light."*

The driver replies, *"Don't worry. My brother does it all the time."*

So they keep driving and they come to a second red light. The driver again puts his foot to the floor and whizzes past the light.

His pal is furious. *"You just went through another red light. What are you playing at?"*

The driver repeats, *"Don't worry. My brother does it all the time."*

The car comes to a third red light and whizzes through.

The driver's friend screams, *"You're going to get us killed! Pull over and let me out."*

The driver shouts back, *"I'm telling you: don't worry. My brother does it all the time."*

So they keep driving and come to a green light. The driver slams on the brakes.

His friend looks at him and says, *"Are you out of your mind? What is wrong with you? You go flying past three red lights, almost getting us killed, and then you slam on the brakes when you have a green light?"*

The driver looks at his mate and says, *"I had to stop; my brother might have been coming."*

Your Song

A man is sitting in a pub feeling rather poor. He sees the man next to him pull a wad of fifty pound notes out of his wallet.

He turns to the rich man and says to him, *"I have an amazing talent; I know almost every song that has ever existed."*

The rich man laughs.

The poor man says, *"I am willing to bet you all the money you have in your wallet that I can sing a genuine song with a girl's name of your choice in it."*

The rich man laughs again and says, *"OK, how about my daughter's name, Joanna Armstrong-Miller?"*

The rich man goes home poor. The poor man goes home rich.

So, what song did he sing?

'Happy Birthday'.

The Irreverent Reverend

The Reverend Sydney Smith (1771 – 1845) was one of the founders of the Edinburgh Review and one of the most celebrated wits of his day. He attributed much of his own lively personality to his French blood. His reflections came from sheer high spirits and Sydney was often the butt of his own jokes. Here, he comments on hearing the news that a young Scotsman was about to marry an older lady of great size.

"Going to marry her! Impossible! You mean a part of her; he could not carry her all himself. It would be a case, not of bigamy, but trigamy; the neighbourhood or the magistrates should interfere. There is enough of her to furnish wives for a whole parish. One man marry her! – it is monstrous! You might people a colony with her; or give an assembly with her; or perhaps take your morning's walk round her, always provided there were frequent resting-places, and you were in rude health. I was rash enough once to try walking round her before breakfast, but only got half-way and gave up exhausted. Or you might read the Riot Act and disperse her; in short, you might do anything with her but marry her."

Sydney's jokes were quite without malice, but might raise a few eyebrows today.

The Sound of Silence

A man is driving down the road and his car breaks down near a monastery. He approaches the monastery, knocks on the door, and announces, *"My car has broken down. Do you think I could stay the night?"*

The monks graciously accept him, give him dinner, offer him bed and breakfast for the night, and even repair his car.

As the man tries to fall asleep, he hears a melancholy and beautiful sound; one unlike anything he's experienced before. The exquisite music of the Sirens that almost made Odysseus wreck his ship comes to his mind. He tosses and turns, trying to comprehend what could possibly be making such a seductive noise.

That night, he doesn't sleep.

The next morning, he asks the monks what the sound was, but they say, *"We cannot tell you. You are not a monk."*

Distraught, the man leaves the monastery.

Years later, after never being able to forget that evocative music, the man goes back to the monastery and pleads again for the answer.

The monks reply, *"We can't tell you. You are not a monk."*

The man says, *"If the only way I can find out what is making that beautiful sound is to become a monk, then please, make me a monk."*

The abbot replies, *"You must travel the earth and tell us how many blades of grass there are, and the exact number of grains of sand. When you find these answers, you can become a monk."*

The man sets about his task.

After years of searching, he returns as a grey-haired old fellow and knocks on the door of the monastery. He is taken before an assembly of the monks.

"In my quest to find what makes that beautiful sound, I travelled the earth and have found what you asked for. By design, the world is in a state of perpetual change. Only God knows what you request. All a man can know is himself, and

only then if he is honest and reflective, and willing to shun self-deception."

The abbot replies, "*Congratulations. You now understand the world and may become a monk. We shall show you the way to the mystery of the sacred sound.*"

The monks lead the man to a wooden door, where the abbot says, "*The sound you seek is beyond that door.*" The monks give him the key, and he opens the door. Behind the wooden door is another door, made of stone. The man is provided with the key and he opens the door, only to find another door, made of ruby. And so it transpires that he needs further keys to doors of emerald, silver and gold.

Finally, the group comes to a diamond door. That extraordinary sound is now crystal clear. The monks say, "*Here is the key to the final door.*"

The man is apprehensive. The answer to his life's quest lies beyond this door. With trembling hands, he unlocks it, turns the handle, and slowly pushes the door open. Falling to his knees, he is dumbfounded to discover the origin of that haunting and wonderful music…

But, I can't tell you, because you're not a monk.

Conundrum I

If a cork is put into a glass of water, the cork will float, and almost always drift to the side of the glass. Using only the cork, glass and water, how can you persuade the cork to float in the middle?

CONUNDRUMS EXPLAINED

Conundrum A

In genealogy, this apparent absurdity is called 'pedigree collapse'. The paradox is explained by shared ancestors. Instead of consisting of different individuals, a family tree may have multiple places occupied by a single person. This typically happens when the parents of an ancestor are related to each other (sometimes unrecognised by themselves). For example, the offspring of two first cousins have at most only six great-grandparents instead of the normal eight.

Small, isolated populations such as those of remote islands represent extreme examples of pedigree collapse, but the common historical tendency to marry those within walking distance, due to the relative immobility of the population before modern transport, meant that most marriage partners were at least distantly related. Even in America, around the nineteenth century, the trend of immigrants to marry among their ethnic, language or cultural group produced many cousin marriages.

Conundrum B

The van and birds will weigh the same no matter what the birds are doing inside.

A common, but mistaken argument, is that when in-flight the birds are not touching anything, they cannot contribute any weight. However, to become airborne the pigeons flap their wings to gain lift. This upwards force must impart an equal downwards force on the air. In turn, this transfers momentum to the bottom of the van, which equals the weight of the birds. This is consistent with Newton's third law of motion, which states that every force has an equal and opposite force. The birds can't go up unless the air goes down.

However, as with most scientific truths, the devil is in the detail. Experiments with sensitive weighing equipment reveal that birds do indeed generate a vertical force equal to their body weight when they flap their wings downwards, but they generate almost no vertical force when they flap their wings upwards – meaning they are effectively weightless. Therefore, if all the birds in the van were to synchronise the flapping of their wings, then the van would have to support twice the weight of the birds during their downstrokes. In practice, of course, the birds tend to flap their wings at different times, meaning the pigeon cargo will, on average, maintain a stable weight.

Conundrum C

This is a popular trick question. A mirror merely reflects what is directly in front of it. It does not reverse left and right; it reverses front to back. Try some simple experiments. Take a mirror (not an heirloom) and a space (preferably away from the family). Look at yourself in the mirror. Point to one side. You and your image are pointing in the same direction. Now point upwards. Again you and your mirror image are pointing in the same direction. However, if you point to the front, your mirror image is pointing in the opposite direction to you. You can try the same experiments standing sideways to the mirror or by placing the mirror on the floor and standing on it. In all cases, the direction reverses only when you point towards or away from the mirror. A common, but misleading, experiment is to write on a card and hold this in front of the mirror, with the writing facing the mirror. The reflection shows the writing has reversed. But, in this case YOU have reversed the writing – by the way you are holding the card. Try writing on a transparent plastic sheet and hold this in front of you so that you can read the writing – no reversal.

So why do we perceive that the mirror flips left and right? This is because we mentally map the mirror image to something that makes physical sense. The front-to-back reversal is mentally interpreted as a 180-degree rotation (something that people do all the time), and a left-to-right reversal (which people don't do, but since our bodies have a strong left-right symmetry, it doesn't seem as strange).

Your mirror image hasn't been swapped left and right, but inverted along a third dimension, like a glove being turned inside out. This is not something commonly experienced (except in science fiction films).

Conundrum D

A tetrahedron, or triangular-based pyramid. Three Beatles are easy to visualise – the shape of an equilateral triangle. Placing a fourth point that is equidistant from the first three points requires moving into the third dimension. Fortunately, there were only four Beatles.

Conundrum E

The puzzle relates to the key signatures of the major scales in music. The number refers to the black notes on the piano keyboard. In the scale of A major there are 3 sharps; in F major there is 1 flat; etc. G major contains one sharp note, so the answer is g = 1.

Conundrum F

Yes. It does not matter what Jill's marital status is.

Conundrum G

Pick up the second glass from the left and pour its contents into the fifth glass in the row. Then return this glass to its original position.

Conundrum H

1. 13%. Suppose one party wins no votes at all in 324 seats but wins each of the other 326 by a single vote, with the other three parties all securing the same number of votes. Then its total vote is one vote over 25% in each of 50.15% of the seats (326 out of 650). This is fractionally over 12.5% of the total vote.
2. 75%. The party wins 324 seats with 100% of the vote. This gives it 49.85% of the total national vote. In the other 326, it is defeated by one vote by another party, with the remaining two parties winning no votes. This is one vote under 50% in 50.15% of the seats – or close to 25% of the national vote.

Conundrum I

The reason that a cork drifts to the side of a glass is that it floats to the highest point. Since water is attracted by the glass, the highest point is around the edge of the water. To get the cork to float in the middle of the glass, all you must do is fill the glass as much as possible. The water will form a convex shape above the glass, with the highest point at its centre. This is where the cork will settle.

Try this for yourself: required are an uncorked bottle of wine (there is no need to consume the contents), an empty beer glass and some water. Cut a one centimetre section from the end of the cork, otherwise it will be too large for the glass.